ALSO IN THE MODERN LIBRARY EXPLORATION SERIES

The Shameless Diary of an Explorer

Mt. McKinley, 20,300 feet, from the northwest, valley of the Tatlatbna River, Kuskokwim watershed, August 15, 1903.

ROBERT DUNN

THE SHAMELESS DIARY OF AN EXPLORER

A Story of Failure on Mt. McKinley

JON KRAKAUER

SERIES EDITOR

Introduction by Edward Hoagland

THE MODERN LIBRARY

NEW YORK

2001 Modern Library Paperback Edition

Introduction copyright © 2001 by Edward Hoagland
Series introduction copyright © 1999 by Jon Krakauer
Biographical note copyright © 2001 by Random House, Inc.

Library of Congress Cataloging-in-Publication Data
Dunn, Robert, 1877–1955.
The shameless diary of an explorer: a story of failure on Mt. McKinley /
Robert Dunn—Modern Library pbk. ed.
p. cm.
ISBN 0-679-78325-3
1. Dunn, Robert, 1877–1955—Diaries. 2. McKinley, Mount (Alaska)—
Discovery and exploration. 3. McKinley, Mount (Alaska)—
Description and travel. 4. Explorers—Alaska—McKinley,
Mount—Diaries. 5. Geologists—United States—Diaries.
6. Mountaineering—Alaska—McKinley, Mount.
7. Cook, Frederick Albert, 1865–1940.
I. Title

F912.M2 D9 2001
917.98'3—dc21   2001030829

Modern Library website address: www.modernlibrary.com

ROBERT DUNN

Robert Steed Dunn, a globe-trotting explorer and journalist during the early years of the twentieth century, was born on August 16, 1877, in Newport, Rhode Island. He came from an old-line patrician family who asked to be removed from the original *Social Register* because it listed such upstarts as the Vanderbilts. Dunn first acquired a passion for exploration and outdoor adventure on boyhood camping trips in the New Hampshire woods. Upon graduating from Harvard, cum laude, in 1898, he headed for the Yukon territory to take part in the Klondike gold rush. Afterward he found work as a cub reporter on the *New York Commercial Advertiser,* then under the editorship of muckraker Lincoln Steffens. "Dunn could write and Dunn could bite, and he bit and wrote his way through with us for months," Steffens recounted in his *Autobiography* (1931). In 1902, Dunn was one of the first journalists to reach the Caribbean island of Martinique after the deadly eruption of Mt. Pelée. The following year, Steffens arranged for him to accompany Dr. Frederick Cook, the controversial polar explorer, on an expedition to scale Mt. McKinley, the highest peak in North America.

The Shameless Diary of an Explorer, Dunn's forthright account of the failed journey, was published in 1907. "Dunn simply could not lie," Steffens later recalled. "Pencil in hand, this born artist had to report things as they were.... I had seen a good deal of arctic explorers, read their books, and heard their gossip, which revealed to me that no book in that field had told it all; they all left out the worst of the wranglings and depressions which were an essential part of the truth about human nature in such tests. Dunn...wrote what I regard as a classic on exploration."

In 1903, while on the Cook expedition, Dunn was credited with discovering and naming Mt. Hunter in the McKinley Range. Three years later, he climbed the newly risen volcanic island of Perry in the Bering Sea and discovered a group of craters at Mt. Okmok in the Aleutian Islands. In 1908, he led the first ascent of Mt. Wrangell in Alaska, and in 1913 he journeyed to Siberia to explore the Kamchatka River. *The Youngest World,* a novel inspired by his Alaskan adventures, came out in 1914.

Dunn also served as a war correspondent. In 1904, he covered the Russo-Japanese War for a New York newspaper and became friends with Jack London. The two met again in the spring of 1914 while reporting on the landing of United States forces in Vera Cruz. With the outbreak of World War I, Dunn headed to Europe for the New York *Evening Post* and recorded his experiences in *Five Fronts* (1915). In 1916, he returned to Mexico for the New York *Tribune* to file stories on General John J. Pershing's expedition aimed at capturing Pancho Villa. Though past the age of enlistment, Dunn joined the Navy when America entered World War I in 1917. Following a stint aboard a destroyer searching out German U-boats in the North Atlantic, he was commissioned a lieutenant and served as an intelligence officer at the United States Naval Headquarters in London. From 1919 to 1922, Dunn was assigned to the United States High Commissioner in Constantinople, where as a staff intelligence aide he played an intriguing Eric Ambler–esque role in Near East politics.

Though Dunn subsequently retired to his home in Katonah, New York, devoting himself to horticulture and writing (*Horizon Fever,* a largely autobiographical novel chronicling the life and adventures of a war correspondent named Rupert Stark, appeared in 1932), during World War II he returned to Turkey to serve as an assistant naval attaché. A volume of his poetry, *And Least Love,* was published in 1945.

Robert Dunn died after a long illness on December 24, 1955, and was buried in Newport. His autobiography, *World Alive,* appeared the following year. *The New York Times Book Review* praised the memoir as a "wide-ranging and free-wheeling odyssey ... the story of a man of independent and often unorthodox opinions, a man bent on adventure and ready to face the dangers and hardships that adventure brings."

Introduction to the Modern Library Exploration Series

Jon Krakauer

Why should we be interested in the jottings of explorers and adventurers? This question was first posed to me twenty-five years ago by a skeptical dean of Hampshire College upon receipt of my proposal for a senior thesis with the dubious title "Tombstones and the Mooses Tooth: Two Expeditions and Some Meandering Thoughts on Climbing Mountains." I couldn't really blame the guardians of the school's academic standards for thinking I was trying to bamboozle them, but in fact I wasn't. Hoping to convince Dean Turlington of my scholarly intent, I brandished an excerpt from *The Adventurer,* by Paul Zweig:

> The oldest, most widespread stories in the world are adventure stories, about human heroes who venture into the myth-countries at the risk of their lives, and bring back tales of the world beyond men.... It could be argued ... that the narrative art itself arose from the need to tell an adventure; that man risking his life in perilous encounters constitutes the original definition of what is worth talking about.

Zweig's eloquence carried the day, bumping me one step closer to a diploma. His words also do much to explain the profusion of titles in bookstores these days about harrowing outdoor pursuits. But even as the literature of adventure has lately enjoyed something of a popular revival, several classics of the genre have inexplicably remained out of print. The Modern Library Exploration Series is intended to rectify some of these oversights.

The ten books we have selected for the series thus far span fifteen centuries of derring-do. All are gripping reads, but they also offer a fascinating look at the shifting rationales given by explorers over the ages in response to the inevitable question: Why would anyone willingly subject himself to such unthinkable hazards and hardships?

In the sixth century, according to medieval texts, an Irish monk known as Saint Brendan the Navigator became the first European to reach North America. Legend has it that he sailed from Ireland to Newfoundland in a diminutive boat sewn from leather hides—a voyage of more than 3,000 miles across some of the world's deadliest seas, purportedly to serve God. *The Brendan Voyage* describes modern adventurer Tim Severin's attempt to duplicate this incredible pilgrimage, in 1976, in an exact replica of Saint Brendan's ancient oxhide vessel—professedly to demonstrate that the monk's journey was not apocryphal.

La Salle and the Discovery of the Great West, by the incomparable prose stylist Francis Parkman, recounts the astonishing journeys of Robert Cavelier, Sieur de La Salle, as he crisscrossed the wilds of seventeenth-century America in hopes of discovering a navigable waterway to the Orient. La Salle did it, ostensibly at least, to claim new lands for King Louis XIV and to get rich. He succeeded on both counts—his explorations of the Mississippi Basin delivered the vast Louisiana Territory into the control of the French crown—but at no small personal cost: In 1687, after spending twenty of his forty-three years in the hostile wilderness of the New

World, La Salle was shot in the head by mutinous members of his own party, stripped naked, and left in the woods to be eaten by scavenging animals.

Weird and Tragic Shores, by Chauncey Loomis, is the story of Charles Francis Hall, a flamboyant Cincinnati businessman and self-styled explorer who, in 1871, endeavored to become the first person to reach the North Pole. Hall, Loomis tells us, was "impelled by a sense of personal destiny and of religious and patriotic mission," and displayed "energy, will power, and independence remarkable even in a nineteenth-century American." He got closer to the pole than any Westerner ever had, but perished en route under mysterious circumstances and was "buried so far north of the magnetic pole that the needle of a compass put on his grave points southwest." In 1968 Loomis journeyed to this distant, frozen grave, exhumed the corpse, and performed an autopsy that cast macabre new light on how Hall came to grief.

Farthest North is a first-person narrative by the visionary Norse explorer Fridtjof Nansen, who in 1893 set sail for the North Pole from Norway with a crew of twelve in a wooden ship christened the *Fram,* hoping to succeed where Hall and so many others had failed. Nansen's brilliant plan, derided as crazy by most of his peers, was to allow the *Fram* to become frozen into the treacherous pack ice of the Arctic Ocean, and then let prevailing currents carry the icebound ship north across the pole. Two years into the expedition, alas, and still more than 400 miles from his objective, Nansen realized that the drifting ice was not going to take the *Fram* all the way to the pole. Unfazed, he departed from the ship with a single companion and provisions for 100 days, determined to cover the remainder of the distance by dogsled and on skis, with no prospect of reuniting with the *Fram* for the return journey. The going was slow, perilous, and exhausting, but they got to within 261 statute miles of the pole before giving up and beginning a desperate, year-long trudge back to civilization.

Unlike La Salle, Hall and Nansen couldn't plausibly defend their passion for exploration by claiming to do it for utilitarian ends. The North Pole was an exceedingly recondite goal, a geographical abstraction surrounded by an expanse of frozen sea that was of no apparent use to anybody. Hall and Nansen proffered what had by then become the justification de rigueur for jaunts to the ends of the earth—almighty science—but it didn't really wash.

Robert Falcon Scott, Nansen's contemporary, also relied on the scientific rationale to justify his risky exploits, and it rang just as hollow. *The Last Place on Earth,* by English historian Roland Huntford, is the definitive, utterly riveting account of the race for the South Pole, which Scott lost to Nansen's protégé, Roald Amundsen, in 1911—and which cost Scott his life, as well. In death, Scott was mythologized as the preeminent tragic hero in the history of the British Empire, but Huntford's book—lauded by *The New York Times* as "one of the great debunking biographies"—portrays him as an inept bungler unworthy of such deification. Huntford also reveals that while Scott was marching toward his demise in Antarctica, his wife, Kathleen, was consummating an affair with his rival's mentor, Nansen, in a Berlin hotel room.

Half a year after Scott met his end, Valerian Albanov joined a Russian expedition that intended to sail from Alexandrovsk (present-day Murmansk) to Vladivostok through the ice-choked waters north of Siberia. Just seven weeks after leaving port, however, their ship was beset by ice in the Kara Sea. Eighteen months later, with supplies running low and the vessel still hopelessly trapped, Albanov led thirteen companions across the vastness of the frozen ocean, on foot and in jerry-built kayaks, in a grim struggle for their lives. Only two men survived the ordeal, one of them being Albanov. His account of the journey, *In the Land of White Death,* is one of the most amazing books ever written about polar exploration.

In *Starlight and Storm,* the dashing French mountaineer Gaston Rébuffat recalls his ascents of the six great north faces of the Alps, including the notorious Eiger Nordwand, during the years following World War II. An incorrigible romantic, he describes his climbs in luminous, mesmerizing prose that is likely to inspire even dedicated flat-landers to pick up an ice ax and light out for the great ranges. And how does Rébuffat reconcile the sport's matchless pleasures with its potentially lethal consequences? He resorts to bald-faced denial: "The real mountaineer," he insists, "does not like taking risks" and shuns danger. Although he acknowledges that in certain unavoidable situations "a thrill runs through him," Rébuffat quickly (and unconvincingly) avows that it is "much too unpleasant a thrill for him to seek it out or to enjoy it."

Walter Bonatti, an Italian contemporary of Rébuffat, was the greatest mountaineer of his era, and among the greatest of any era. His ascents in the Alps and the Himalaya set an almost unimaginably audacious standard that modern climbers still aspire to. In *The Mountains of My Life*, Bonatti recounts all the highlights of his dazzling alpine career, but he devotes special attention to the first ascent of K2, the world's second-highest mountain, in 1954. Bonatti was the unsung hero of this monumental achievement, yet afterward he was slandered and vilified by many of his teammates and countrymen. In these pages, for the first time in English, we are given a revealing, in-depth account of the K2 climb and its bitter aftermath from Bonatti's perspective.

The peculiar individuals who populate *Great Exploration Hoaxes*, by David Roberts, were no less driven to make a mark than Bonatti, or Nansen, or La Salle. But whereas the latter all deserved their renown, nine of the ten adventurers featured in Roberts's book achieved their fame through breathtaking acts of deceit. Interestingly, several of these fraudulent explorers were fierce rivals of men profiled in this series. In the late 1950s, for instance, Cesare Maestri was engaged in a race with Bonatti to make the first ascent of a spectacular South American peak called Cerro Torre, then considered the most difficult mountain on earth. After failing to reach the summit, Maestri claimed it anyway, perpetrating an elaborate fraud that still reverberates through the world mountaineering community.

One of the more memorable liars portrayed in *Great Exploration Hoaxes* is Dr. Frederick Cook, who falsely insisted that he was both the first person to reach the North Pole and the first to stand atop Mt. McKinley, at 20,320 feet the highest peak in North America. It's unfortunate that Cook resorted to such colossal deceits, because his résumé included a number of genuinely laudable accomplishments. Indeed, in 1903, three years before his fake ascent of McKinley, Cook led a six-man expedition that completed the first circumnavigation of the massive Alaskan mountain—a grueling, 540-mile odyssey that would not be repeated for seventy-five years.

The unofficial chronicler of Cook's 1903 McKinley expedition was a young Harvard graduate with literary ambitions named Robert Dunn, whose intriguing, shockingly candid book, *The Shameless Diary of an Explorer,* broke fresh ground in the literature of exploration. Previously, expedition narratives were conspicuously devoid of passages that presented participants in an unflattering light. But Dunn told it like it really was, with considerable skill, and feelings be damned. His brutal honesty and biting wit make for an enthralling read.

If none of the extraordinary people featured in these chronicles adequately answers the nagging question—What drove you to take such risks?—perhaps it is simply because adventurers, on the whole, are congenitally averse to leading examined lives. "If you have to ask," they like to mumble by way of dodging their inquisitors, "you just wouldn't understand." Rest assured, however, that the convolutions of the adventurous psyche are richly illuminated in these ten compelling volumes, however enigmatic the protagonists may have remained to themselves.

INTRODUCTION

Edward Hoagland

Just as we sing Caruso-like arias in the shower, many of us have fantasized about embarking on far-flung adventures—a Himalayan rafting trip down the Brahmaputra River, or clambering near its headwaters where nobody has ever climbed before. Operas in the sky. One thing that holds us back, besides a sensible fear of hunger, cold, and broken bones, and the tedium of first planning and then slogging to the jump-off point, is that we know our companions would probably not wear well. And when we read collegial firsthand accounts of "conquering" nature, summiting this or that tremendous peak or sailing endlessly between icebergs, we'll usually feel as though the narrator is not telling the truth: his companions didn't get along *that* well.

Also, to a contemporary sensibility, so much of outdoor dare-devilry seems to treat nature as merely gym machinery. I meet people who have climbed Mt. Kilimanjaro without ever bothering to inquire what tribe the men who lug their baggage belong to. The garbage littering parts of Mt. Everest is an international scandal, and I've stayed in Talkeetna, the village under Mt. McKinley in

Alaska, and listened all day to the silly roar of planes or helicopters flying as close to the top as aircraft can routinely land, to keep aspirants' vacation schedules neat and compact.

Even Alaska's eleven-hundred-mile Iditarod sled-dog race, which is not for trippers, was sullied for me one midwinter on the Yukon River when I witnessed how an actual winner trained his team. He fed his dogs on the dogs that "didn't make the cut." That is, on a practice run, he would unhook the dogs from the traces, if he didn't think they were pulling hard enough, and shoot the laggards with a pistol in front of the other dogs, throw the corpses on the sled to freeze, chain-saw them into sections when he got home in a couple of hours, and then boil them—bones and hair and all—to feed to the survivors. (He bought dead dogs from the local Indians to supplement his own supply.) Other team owners I met joked about their own "gunfights at the O.K. Corral," when they might slaughter half a kennel of sled dogs—though, like the Indians, they regarded making the dogs that were left eat the executed animals as "bad medicine."

I once climbed Mt. Katahdin, in Maine, and at twenty glissaded down Mt. Jefferson, in Oregon, but now prefer to gaze upward at a massif and pretend that it never has been, and never will be, scaled. This book, *The Shameless Diary of an Explorer,* is from the era when triumphalism was not gymnastic, however, and McKinley—"the pivot of the world," as the author grandiosely described it in 1903—was still uncharted. Therefore, his motley, almost accidental crew set out to win the fame of topping it. (Denali, as McKinley is now often called, wasn't climbed by Native Americans, because—like other tribal peoples worldwide—they tended to leave each peak in peace as a spirit-world, just as they seldom killed big game gratuitously or without a propitiating ceremony.) The expedition's leader, Frederick Cook—"the Professor," as Robert Dunn contemptuously labels him—had failed in New York City as a medical doctor, and not many years later would achieve notoriety by falsely claiming to be the first man to reach the North Pole. (He had already falsely said in 1906 that on a second expedition he had succeeded in climbing McKinley. Eventually, Cook was to serve five years in federal prison for mail fraud.) Dunn himself, at twenty-six, is a journalist, a protégé of the pioneering muckraker Lincoln Steffens, and a former 1898 Gold Rush stampeder, a Harvard graduate, and a sparkling descriptive writer who seems to have mulled over and memorized, while trudging the trail all day long, the words that would go into his diary.

"Simon," also from New York, is a dilettante botanist, age twenty-one, heir to a paint fortune, and much made fun of as a Jew by the anti-Semitic Dunn, who, being a true gentleman of his time, scants the Irish as well and refers to all Indians as "Siwashes." The expedition picks up a good horse wrangler from Montana and an eager office worker in Seattle to serve as photographer, and an unemployed prospector is shanghaied from an Alaskan island where their ferryboat happens to stop. Then there are the fifteen suffering horses, shipped in from Washington State and beaten constantly and mercilessly until at last their usefulness is over and they are abandoned to the wolves.

These nature lovers, like so many outdoorsmen, love only rocks or flowers or some other special wedge of the entire pie (like pet owners who compartmentalize their feeling for animals to exclude anything that's wild). Yet Dunn is free of the braggadocio and winsome ingratiation that plague other adventurers' books. Instead, his maverick irascibility is appealing, and the vertiginous landscapes, shot through with braided cataracts and layered light, all get their vivid due. This is the first known circumnavigation of the mountain—a feat not repeated until 1978—and the route up which they half-ascended, via the Peters Glacier, was not completely conquered till 1954. Dunn does it lasting justice, while putting in the messy squabbles, the seams of cruelty and folly, and their feckless, secretive leader, the Professor, with his wrongly sighted rifle and a theodolite he didn't know how to use, who sloughs off the shanghaied prospector like a busted boot about midway, with a pittance of food and the lamest horse, when he falls sick with pleurisy, to survive just if he can.

Alfred Brooks, the government geologist for whom the Brooks Range is named, had explored much of their path in a survey trek the previous year, and various gold-seekers had made the grizzlies, moose, and caribou already timid ahead of these "bourgeois and cranks," as Dunn characterizes the party—Simon wearing a moose's dewlap for a cap when not clubbing the horses unpardonably. But Dunn ends up apologizing to him for quarreling, and wonders in his diary: "Shall I ever return to so glorious a land, to such happiness?" And if you read about how shabbily Admiral Robert Peary—Frederick Cook's monumental rival for that North Pole first—exploited the Greenland Eskimos, you may forgive Cook's round-the-bend ego. These vain and fishy, famously obsessive, brutal explorers, like Henry Stanley in Africa, could verge on the psychotic even in success. Stanley's naturalist on an 1888 expedition, an Englishman named James Jameson, once paid "six handkerchiefs" to have an eleven-year-old slave girl led out of a hut, tied to a tree, and then stabbed, skinned, butchered, washed for the pot, and cooked and eaten by the villagers, so that he could sketch the whole process.

Recently an ecologist, for conservation purposes, walked a twelve-hundred-mile transect across some of the densest Congo/Gabon jungle left to be examined. But he broke his progress and sacrificed a stretch of data in order to see to the welfare of a sick pygmy in his party—and he was never "attacking" nature, like the turn-of-the-last-century explorers and mountaineers, but trying to save it. So we must loop back to that more lavish and yet terse era, when rich men assumed as their birthright the privilege of filling in the map's blank spaces, like this roof of the continent, telling God that there was nothing He could create they couldn't stand atop. (Eleven attempts at McKinley were mounted during Dunn's decade alone, until an Anglican bishop, appropriately, made the conquest.) The sort of privacy we may still enjoy at precious moments along the Susitna, the Tanana, and Kuskokwim rivers, draining the great massif, was then whole-cloth and wholesale. And Dunn, if you read his memoir, *World Alive,* published half a century later, was probably never happier. After journalism, he led a checkered career in military intelligence—he describes, for instance, administering a lengthy water torture to a Mexican revolutionary. Cook, too, was mired almost ever afterward in acrid activities and controversies. Nor is the wild Kuskokwim lately a happier place. A night I spent in the village of Sleetmute during the 1980s was punctuated by the gunfire of feuding Indian families. Then, on New Year's Day, downriver in the Eskimo community of Crooked Creek, I stumbled on a medium-size dog lying frozen in front of his owners' cabin, where he had been thrown after his hind legs had been chopped off during the night's festivities. In another town, a nurse from the Lower 48, who was putting in a year's assignment on the Kuskokwim, told me that she had just broken up with a local lover, but that he had begun avenging himself by shooting all of her dog team from hiding places up in the spruces on the ridge top— one a day, or one by one. She was weeping. She couldn't keep them indoors all the time.

Yet Alaska still has wolves and lynx and wood frogs. And for a corrective to *The Shameless Diary of an Explorer,* you might want to read John Muir's *Travels in Alaska* (he made three trips between 1879 and 1890). Meanwhile, the results of the obliteration of nature— both as a mystery and as an obstacle—diffuse the violence with which we once attacked it upon our domestic lives and upon ourselves, at the same time as that new void dissolves the ancient links we'd kept with one another in order to face down the mysteries and obstacles. But this is a splendid chronicle of the jumbo, primeval Alaska, circa 1903, when it began to be in flux: and a curio resurrected from an obscurity such a book never deserved.

————

EDWARD HOAGLAND is the author of nearly twenty books, several of which have been nominated for the National Book Award, the American Book Award, and the National Book Critics Circle Award. A member of the American Academy of Arts and Letters, Hoagland lives in Bennington, Vermont.

CONTENTS

Maps

ILLUSTRATIONS

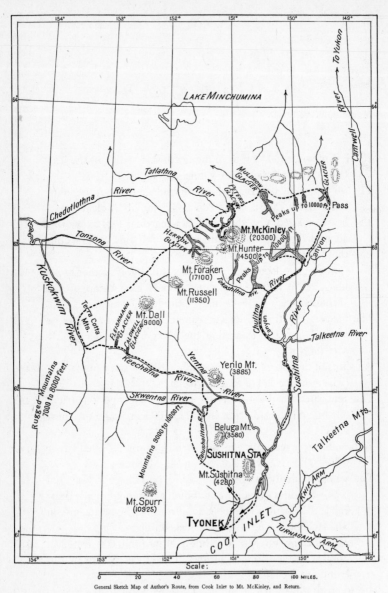

General Sketch Map of Author's Route, from Cook Inlet to Mt. McKinley, and Return.

General Sketch Map

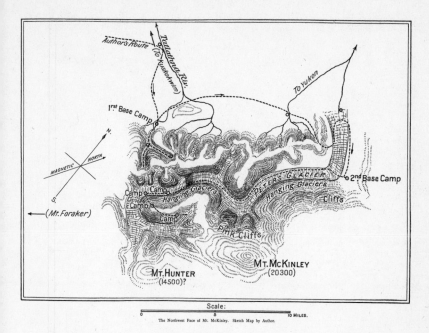

Northwest Face Map

THE SHAMELESS
DIARY OF AN
EXPLORER

CHAPTER I

THE MASTER MOTIVE

This is the story of a failure. I think that success would have made it no more worth telling. It is about an exploring party, the sort that so often fails....

Fountains of youth, or eldorados, or wider realms for cross and conscience—these seemed to lure a younger world to unknown regions. To-day men explore for the iron crown of science; they say that they do, at least.

But I believe that neither biology to-day, nor gold nor the creeds of old, have ever been the explorer's master motive. His real ardor is more profound. It has revealed and civilized our sphere. It stirs the thirst to discover and subdue which vests the very fiber of our race; makes us ache for tumult and change, for strife for its own sake against big odds. The true spirit of the explorer is a primordial restlessness. It is spurred by instincts of pre-natal being and a cloudy hereafter, to search the glamour of unknown peaks and seas and forests for assurance of man's imperfect faith in immortality. It is a creative instinct.

The explorer seldom speaks of it openly; he is not unwilling, but he cannot. He is inarticulate, like the victim of a passion. Few but he can understand his inspiration. The world asks of him purposes more obvious. He cites a widespread fervor; of old, perhaps religion; to-day, he will name science. And these are or have been his impulses, in part; and the world can grasp them. Science is the natural heir to the cross as the public avatar of exploration. Each is sponsor for the Unknowable; one was, one is now, the Aladdin lamp of the Improbable.

But science is a cold ambition, remoter from our master motive than the world's old notions of exploration, vain as they would seem to-day were they not dead in us. Maybe no peaks remain, flushed with the light that forswears mortality; no unknown seas to shatter doubt with wonder. That I do not believe. For men still roam over a world too wide for any map, and when restlessness and action for its own sake inspire us no more, our race will deserve to die.

All reverence to science! Yet I know this: The elder explorers related what quickened the life and visions of their time, and quickens ours, rousing men to ever harder ventures. Few who seek the iron crown stir us so now. Few men in the street see the "use" of exploration, in the North, especially. To many, explorers seem vain men seeking short cuts to fame, or persons who waste time, energy, and wealth, to win the Impossible, to learn the Unprofitable. And this cynicism appears to be not all the fault of laymen's apathy, or of explorers' dumbness.

If the earth is smaller and tamer than in the old days, our sympathies are warmer and the whole world's heart is more alert. It craves, above all, knowledge of itself, for it is a more complex and interesting old world. The life of man as it is, naked and unshadowed, brutal maybe, life under every stress of fortune—*that* wins the hungry ear and the deeper charity of these present hours. And life has thus been searched and exploited almost everywhere all lands over, except: Among us who seek on enchanted rivers an answer to those under-thoughts that make life at once a tragic and an ecstatic thing, who dare for nothing but the cause of daring, who follow the long trails.

Men with the masks of civilization torn off, and struggling through magic regions ruled over by the Spirit of the North or of the South; human beings tamed by the centuries, then cast out to shift for themselves like the first victims of existence—they must offer the best field of all to help this knowledge of ourselves. He knows life best who has seen it nakedest, and most exotic. So he that goes plainspoken from the city to the outer waste should become indeed quite wise. He might tell how the weakling's eyes blazed with courage and reproach when his leader turned back disheartened, or in what words the athlete of the avenue may be the first to whimper at starvation; and men would sit up and see some of their children in a very, very large perspective. And in telling the truth about others, a man might reveal it about himself, which would be best of all.

The passions of the long trail bring out the best in men and the worst, and all in scarlet; and while the law of compensation, which keeps life livable, provides that in the after-memories which form existence, only what is pleasant survives, I hold that it is unfair to nature and the blessed weaknesses which make us human to divert by one hair's breadth in any record of the trail from facts as you saw them, emotions as you felt them at their time. To distort or hide, in deference to any custom, or so-called sense of pride or honor, simply is to lie. The tragic moments in the heat of the trail's struggle, *the event as it affected you as you then were*—to note that with all the passion or heroism, the beastliness or triumph, of the moment—must not such a record in the end turn out all fair? And true as can be?

Exactly this honesty explorers to-day do *not* attempt. From their stories I get in my mouth a horrid taste of varnish. Modestly they derogate all heroism or cowardice in the outer places, and dryly, oh, how dryly! Whatever may beget that big perspective, that in particular is hidden—the while from the borders of beyond you hear rumors of quarrels on the floe, of heroic forbearance, of trivial impatience. But never a living man or human act! And little science, either. A conclusion relates: The real results of this expedition will appear during the next ten years, one volume a year, printed in Latin by the society that financed us.

I do not accuse science directly of this concealment; only, science is the link between the world and the explorer, the key to what he gives it in answer to its encouragement and its instinctive interest in him. But it surely seems to me that the modern explorer deliberately avoids illuminating the world in a corner which is very dark, which he knows best. Wherein, after and beyond all others, he has chance to tell the greatest human truths, he has to all intents—deceived. If he is pledged to exactitude about his diptera, is he not obliged, in relating human deeds at all, to record as truthfully and in full how the outer waste and the ego of each companion uplifted or scarred his own? Is not this human obligation the greater one, in justice to the explorer's self as stirred by his master motive, and to the world whose encouragement unwittingly has the same source? If such a record be not as direct, as full, as frank, as his registry in science, by what hypocrisy under the sun has he right to state at all the words or acts of any fellow?

But when I proposed to reveal life as I saw it in the back of beyond, in order to realize something of that large perspective, I was met with silence, or cant. It was against the custom of exploration; it would harm the business, destroy order and discipline. It wasn't loyal to one's companions in the battle of the trail to record words and acts for which their saner selves were not responsible; and besides, much happened in the outer places which the world had better not know, said some explorers. Everywhere I encountered the inhuman repression which one associates with science; not with that experimental science of the daring and uplifting imagination, but with that jealous sort that disputes and differentiates—a justification for deeds of inspiration, not their honest end. Loyalty to truth was gaped at. Apart from malice, such an idea was inconceivable to these persons.

Disloyal? To be insincere is disloyalty. Human nature in the large is concrete; men are responsible beings, wherever in the world, at whatever task—else we have no need of law, and the insane expert must rule us. It is insincere to deny a man responsibility for his acts, dishonorable to pervert by gloss or omission the significance of any of his deeds, noble or ignoble.

Custom and false standards of honor have stultified exploration. To-day the world dwells mostly on the sensational fact of winning pole or peak, oblivious that the long human struggle, inspired by that master motive which mitigates endurance and suffering, are to the explorer his real end, consciously or not. Although it needs aid from a liberal world, exploration in the true sense never was or can be a business; and order and discipline are primarily vested in the force of honest and inspired personalities. Viewed thus, it is hypocrisy to accuse outspokenness with malice. And *what*, to-day, I ask, had the world better not know?

———

This Diary is an attempt to give, perhaps for the first time, a glimpse of that large perspective. Yet I went on this expedition through Alaska with no such idea in mind. I started and maintained my record with the sole idea of stating facts as I saw them, emotions as I felt them at their time. Only after the job was all done did its meaning show clear.

Maybe it has been a shameless task. I know that it is without malice. For heaven's sake do not read these pages with charity. Its words as they appear here were so written at the time that the events and feelings which they represent occurred; if not always in present order, or exact form of sentence, immediately from notes, and on the trail. Only clearness demanded the few insertions, public taste insignificant omissions.

I know that the whole truth is always beyond reach. Sometimes you think that there cannot be such a thing. Utter self-detachment is impossible, and the greater the human strain, the more remote. The tension of the trail casts a shadow over life, could we dispel which we should be gods. To tell the truth about other people is hardest of all. But if you are honest at it, you may reach at least one end: You will have told the truth about yourself. It is beyond the power of words or art to make any one feel exactly as I have felt a-crossing the Alaskan tundra. Afterwards, you seem to have written of stage rivers, stage swamps, property horses; of unreal acts, and words, and shifts of human feature. Under that tension, the human ego, with its warring equations, instincts, race traits, will seem to have distorted brain and hand; added futility to injustice. In the after-comforts of home, you may seem to have libeled companions whom in the field (under that uncontrollable restraint that all men feel beside a fellow with his mask off) you felt sure you gave less than their due. But the vision of which life, afield or by fireside, is the more searching? That in the outer waste, I think.

The journey was no polar dash, no battle with a tropic jungle. It involved no heroic struggle for life, though we were always in utter wilderness. Yet no explorer, knowing the peculiar scourges of summer travel in Alaska, as we had to undertake it, would afford to smile at us. Perhaps we were ill-equipped, incompetent. We did the best we could with the resources at hand. At any rate, our masks of civilization again and again were torn off, and—nakedness is nakedness; and—all in all we tried our hardest. Therein lies fitness enough for an inkling of the large perspective. I know that I am an explorer only potentially, in spirit. I would not presume to try a task harder than this Diary relates.

We failed. Failure is more than the average lot of any venture. It is typical, and through its dark glass human nature appears more colorful and more complex than in the raw light of achievement. So I think that failure, more than less, helps the significance of this record. That our task may since have been accomplished bears not at all upon it. The fiascos could reveal more of the big perspective than the successes of exploration, and give it more honest touch and a brighter future with all men.

We of this journey had no mutual obligations, except those that bind laborers in the same shop. I am under no debt of sentiment or gratitude, subjective or material, to the men of this Diary. How to do each day's work with least friction of limb and soul—that was our one problem. Restraint was imperative overtly on the trail, and there alone was exigent for physical reasons. How each of us helped or hindered the day's work is all my story. We were not friends in any sense admitting sentiment. Yet I believe that I have given, and now give, the men with whom I traveled no reason to be my enemies. I believe that no motives of any sort distort my written record, except the elements of my own temperament and heritages. And I hope that in reporting any inherent vanity in my fellows, I have hit off hardest my own insufferable egotism.

CHAPTER II

GEOGRAPHICAL

Our aim was to reach the top of Mt. McKinley, the highest point of North America, which lifts 20,300 feet of ice over the wastes of west Alaska. This was really a double task. With the means at hand, we knew that to gain the base of the mountain might be hardly easier than to climb it.

A dozen other lands, a dozen other ventures, could have served the purport of this Diary as well. Mt. McKinley and Alaska, as such, are not vital to it. Yet since it does deal with them, their geography must be understood.

Alaska, physically, is more Asiatic than American. Its three main mountain chains run west and east, like all big uplifts in the old world. No northwest-southeast, or northeast-southwest ranges (cordilleras), which are typical of the New World, go west of Lynn Canal, where the Cascade Mountains die and end our systems. The Alaskan alpine region lies entirely south of the Yukon River (which cuts the country in half from east to west), north of which the ranges are lower and chaotic. Alaska is a thumb of Asia, deceivingly detached from it by shallow Behring Sea, which is not a continental boundary. Alaska appears to stick out west from us, while really it hangs eastward from Siberia.

Think of these three ranges as half circles, and you may see alpine Alaska by arranging them thus: To the right, east on the map, place the first segment, so that it bulges to the north. This is the St. Elias–Chugach range, which borders the Pacific Ocean for five hundred miles, from Lynn Canal to the east shore of Cook Inlet, where it ends. To the left, west, place the second, in line with the first segment, but bow it south. This is the Peninsula-Aleutian range, which starts on the west shore of Cook Inlet, and, ridging the Alaskan Peninsula as it points southwest, is submerged to become the Aleutian Islands, which for six hundred miles separate Behring Sea from the Pacific, and all but touch Siberia. Between them runs an arm of the Sea—Cook Inlet—continued north as the valley of a river. But the third arc place thus: To the right, and parallel to the Chugach range, bulging north, but generally two hundred miles inland, and so that it reaches around the sea arm and river valley to touch the Peninsula range at its start. These are the Alaskan Mountains, the greatest sub-arctic chain in the world, and McKinley is its apex. The Sushitna River drains the valley north of the Inlet, forming thus the nearest tidewater route to the great mountain.

McKinley lies at the northernmost point of its range's arc, a few miles west. Approaching from the east, peaks of 10,000 to 12,000 feet touch the big southern tributary of the Yukon, the Tanana. They reach no further toward the Arctic Circle. Here the heights break a little, and Cantwell River eats into them, south from the Tanana. On its west bank, the peaks tower again, quickly lifting McKinley from a 12,000 foot ridge. Now they bear off southwest, with Mount Hunter, 15,000 feet; Mount Foraker, 17,100 feet; Mount Russell, 11,350 feet. And imperceptibly the chain is joined to the Peninsula heights, about the head of the south fork of Kuskokwim River.

Thus, more than fancifully, McKinley is the pivot of the world. By latitude its topmost high mountain, McKinley rises at the middle of that bar of land, Alaska, connecting the two dry masses that form our earth. Southeast it scatters alps toward the Wrangel volcano and our dwarfed cordilleras; southwest strews volcanoes—Iliamna, Pavloff, the new-born Bogosloff isles—till the smoke of Seguam and many another sinks slowly under the sea off Kamchatka.

Cook Inlet is one hundred and fifty miles from McKinley, as the raven flies. From the trading store at Tyonek, on its west shore, the mountain is visible sometimes as a ghostly cap of snow over the Sushitna swamps, and on clear days from far south at sea, on the hill behind the Russian church at Kodiak Island, a tiny golden exhalation. The old explorers, Vancouver, Captain Cook, La Perouse, saw McKinley six score years ago; so did Baron Wrangel, Baranoff, and many a Byzantine Archimandrite. Native Aleut and Kenaitze, with proper awe, called it "Bulshaia" (Russian "bulshoi"—"great") and adventurers, in the first enchanting struggles with gold and death, shrouded it with all camp-fire romance.

Yet none guessed that Bulshaia dwarfed Chimborazo, St. Elias, Orizaba, till Mr. W. A. Dickey, common prospector and Princeton graduate, gave proofs, renaming it McKinley from the Sushitna Valley in 1896. And it was Robert Muldrow of the Geological Survey, following Dickey, who measured the peak in 1898. Captain Herron, lost in the Kuskokwim tundras the next year, approached McKinley and Foraker from the west. But it remained for Alfred H. Brooks of the Geological Survey to reach its base, in 1902. He climbed to about 7,000 feet the outlying range, 10,000 feet high, which separates it from the Yukon-Kuskokwim watershed. I had seen McKinley twice in 1900, from the flank of the Wrangel volcano, and from the Ketchumstock Hills on Forty-mile River in early winter.

Where McKinley rises on the outer periphery of their arc, the Alaskan Mountains are more than forty miles broad, leaping abruptly from the low swamps on either side. The range is ramified like the outspread arms of an octopus by probably the greatest inland glaciers of the world outside the Antarctic continent.

Between actual climbing-base and summit, Mt. McKinley has a greater relief than any other of the world's mountains. It has also the longest snow and ice slope. The real base of McKinley is only 2,600 feet above the sea; perpetual snow line, to which horses can be taken, is at 5,000 feet. Most high mountains give you 7,000 feet, at most, of snow and ice work; McKinley demands 15,000. Excessive glaciation has quickly eroded the uplift into steep amphitheaters with sheer ridges. All glaciers are "hanging" in their upper parts, leaving nowhere a cliff unclothed. Snow slides, snow and rain, are almost incessant. In Alaska, weather conditions are subarctic. Excepting Mt. St. Elias, all big ascents heretofore have been made in temperate, or warmer, regions, from high base camps, reached by pack beasts over solid trails. (Mt. Ruwenzori, too, may be an exception.) Aconcagua, 22,834 feet, was climbed without a foot being placed in snow, from a 14,000-foot base, to which mules were taken. Mustaghata, 25,600 feet, was ascended to 20,600 feet with yaks. Effective height in the Himalayas is even less.

And almost as baffling was the route which we had to take to the base of McKinley. We planned to travel by pack-train from Tyonek, on Cook Inlet, up the western tributaries of the Sushitna, across the Alaskan range to the head of the south fork of the Kuskokwim, and follow along its face northeast to the mountain foot; *i.e.,* to follow the sides of a right angle pointed west, in order to reach a point almost due north of Cook Inlet. This was, in the main, Brook's route, and Herron had followed it in part, although we knew that most traces of their trails would be obliterated. The distance was about 450 miles, and Brooks had covered it with horses in seven weeks from Tyonek. The first half was to be over the tundras of the Sushitna Valley, the remainder across higher ground on the west side of the Alaskan range.

We were forced to travel thus in order to reach the northwest face of the mountain. Brooks had proved it accessible, and it was the side least surrounded by peaks and glaciers. It seemed from every point of view the best from which to ascend. Following up tributaries of the Kuskokwim and Yukon (Tanana) Rivers would have landed us within a hundred miles of this northwest face; but we had neither time nor money to take a pack-train, which was necessary anyhow, to their heads of navigation. By ascending the Sushitna River, we could have reached the southeast side of McKinley, that most thickly insulated by ice and mountains, and worst in climate. Over Brooks' route we might gain the foot of McKinley in the single summer at hand, with a month for recon-noitering and ascents.

I dreaded that first half, the Sushitna tundra. Tundra, strictly speaking, is the coastal marshland of Siberia, yet any vast, low, and ill-drained country in the North, forested or no, is called tundra. It was considered almost madness to venture into the interior over-land from Tyonek. Stories were told of men who had set out from there to be driven back crazed by mosquitoes. I had traveled over tundra in Alaska, and knew its hateful yellow moss bordered by white skeleton spruces, its treacherous ponds sprinkled with white flowers, its willow thickets concealing abysses of red muck. The buzz of bull-dog flies, the hot anger and desperation of burdened cayuses kicking helplessly in a mire, were familiar enough. But I believed that to reach our mountain was just the old, old act of hit-ting the trail, hitting very, very hard, and staying with it.

The ascent seemed to be more doubtful. Ours must be a dash to the top, taking long chances, I thought, on success. Our time for re-connoitering in uncertain weather was too short. McKinley was a very large mountain, quite unexplored, deeply bedded in a great range. St. Elias was not conquered until the fifth try, and then by trained alpine men, at a cost of $50,000. Ours was to be a first at-tempt, by men of no alpine experience, who had hardly $5,000. But the men who had failed on St. Elias declared that alpinists would have succeeded there no better; and I believe that Prof. Russell would have climbed St. Elias if he had had the exceptionally fine weather which brought the Italian Duke of the Abruzzi success there.

But our limitations made me no less eager for the adventure. I longed, at any cost, to return to Alaska, whose hard freedom I have always loved better than anything else on earth.

CHAPTER III

THE OUTFIT,
HUMAN AND MATERIAL

Who we of this expedition were, our measure of fitness for this job—that the Diary should tell. Here is no place to be personal, except on the surface, which is necessary.

The Professor, our leader, was a man of polar experience, hardly versed in the craft of trail or woods, or packing horses. He was our topographer and meteorologist; but the top of McKinley, not science, was our prime object, he told me; and that once we were at the foot, he was certain that the summit would be ours, at the rate of 5,000 feet a day. I believe in looking hardest at the uncertainties of a struggle, not letting the glamour of its sure victories dazzle you. The Professor was more than forty years old; married; of German descent; fair-haired, large-featured.

He chose me as geologist, and to be second in command. I have that fervor for geology, backed by small book knowledge, which blesses all habitual wanderers in the chaotic North. I had been an adventurer on the Edmonton trail to the Klondike in 1898, where a fifth of us died, and two years later had explored the Wrangel volcano, two hundred miles east of McKinley. I was unmarried, twenty-six, Yankee.

Of the four other members of our party, the Professor picked two, and two were casually included on the way to Cook Inlet.

The first I call Simon. He was a Jew. The Professor asked me if I objected on that score to his joining us. I said that I did not. I have the racial, not the religious, repugnance to Jews. I had never relished their race-selfishness, and scouted their tenacity under physical and mental stress. The Diary shows how wrong I was here in one regard, at least. But in my ardor to get North, I persuaded myself that such natural instincts were prejudices, and unworthy. Simon's only adventuring had been with the summer session of a North Polar fiasco, on which he made a collection of flowers. So he was to be our botanist. He was small, dark, rotund, and twenty-one.

Next, was Fred King, of Montana. He had packed the Government horses on Brooks' Geological Survey trip to McKinley. He joined the Professor in eastern Washington, where our leader had picked and bought from Indians fifteen pack-horses, some broken, some unbroken. I first saw him in Seattle. He was a small man, with a fragile forehead and clear eyes; unmarried; in the mid-thirties. He had spent his life packing and trapping in the Bitter Root Mountains. "Would you know about horses?" he asked me when we met. I asked his opinion of our beasts. "Does the Professor know a lot about horses?" he asked again. I said that I did not know. He went on: "I think they'll make the trip, but they're not just the animals I'd have picked."

Though discredited for Alaska, I thought it best to take an alpine guide. We had neither time nor money to send to Europe for one, but we knew that Swiss guides, although with second-class certificates, had been imported into Canada by a railroad. I went to Banff and found that they were not for rent; failed to get one. And the horse-rustlers there said: "You don't want no Swiss guides. They're handy high up on rocks and ice, but lose themselves in the woods. Six weeks across Alasky swamps? They'd die or quit you the first day."

In Seattle we outfitted. I hate it—lists of grub, clothing, saddlery, pots; musing on how neatly this new poncho buckle will free your arm, that cheese-cloth lining make your tent mosquito-proof. We clicked and condemned each neat, new, folding device that will not last a minute on the tundra. We bought, briefly, for grub: Eighty-six pounds per month per man, the government Alaskan ration; mostly flour, beans, bacon, and sugar, with tea, which the climate makes you crave, and little coffee—food least in bulk, greatest in nourishment; sixteen hundred pounds in all, for six men for three months, the least time that we could be on the trail. This is the pioneer-prospectors' fare, taught by experience. We let alone all tinned food, except to pamper ourselves with a few cans of milk and butter; tins give least sustenance in proportion to weight and bulk, pack abominably through soft ground and rough, and we had to travel fast and light. We had no use for patent or condensed grub, except some erbswurst pea-soup—an experiment, though it is German army emergency ration. We counted on killing sheep, moose, and caribou on the north side of the Alaskan range, where King said that they were thick. We took arctic pemmican, two cheeses, and a box of biscuits to eat on the mountain; primus stove, two spirit lamps, wood alcohol and kerosene to cook with above snow line; no stimulant at all—I have never seen and cannot imagine a case in the North where it would be of use—some drugs, I forget which, as we never used them.

Clothing: Boot-rubbers and heavy asbestos-tanned boots for the trail, light boots for the mountain; wool underwear, overalls, jumpers, German socks, rubber sheeting. For the mountain: Four real eiderdown bag-quilts, and much sure-enough arctic dress, hair ropes, ice-axes. For horses: Twelve saw-buck saddles, three Abercrombies, hobbles, cinch-rope, sling rope, oiled pack-covers, a cowbell, and a double blanket and a half for each brute—we slept in these on the trail, taking but one real sleeping-bag. A canvas tent for four; for the mountain, a conical Shantung silk thing, designed by the Professor. Guns: A Savage .3033, the Professor's Greenland .44 Winchester relic, and Simon's arsenal—a Winchester .22 and Colt automatic .38. Instruments: Aneroids, thermometers, Abeny level, but, I think, no sextant or artificial horizon; no mercurial barometer, anyhow, though the Professor filled two huge boxes to torture their pack beast in the name of science.

My scientific outfit went no further than a geological hammer. Other hardware: Heavy steel and granite cook pots, no aluminum— which burns like tallow when grease-soaked; nails, wire, and two axes; my Weno Hawkeye with Goerz double anastigmatic lens, the Professor's reflex camera, a No. 3 Kodak, films in tin cases bound with electric tape, Zeiss field glasses. No chairs or tables; no luxuries at all, not because we posed at roughing it, but because fifteen horses in a new, soft country is quite too big a pack train, anyhow. We bought with an eye to fast, hard, light travel, and that alone. Nothing "patent," nothing "folding," nothing "automatic" but the Colt—and a kind of fire-grid, with legs, to cook over, the Professor's obsession. Something over a ton in all; that seems enough to remember.

Seattle furnished our fifth man, Miller. An utter stranger, he had sought us out and asked us to take him. The Professor twice refused, not admiring his physique; but the night our horses and outfit were loaded on the S.S. *Santa Ana,* for Cook Inlet (June 10, 1903), we still had not enough men. Miller appeared on the dock to see us off—and came with us. He was tall and slim and quiet; a low-voiced youth of twenty-four, who did office work in the Seattle city hall, and was clever with cameras. He was our photographer.

We still needed another man. But at Juneau, Sitka, Yakutat, where we touched, following up the coast, all fit men were either hot on the trail of certain riches, or their dreams of gold had turned to ashes in the mouth, and they were bound home. Glaciers shot bristling into the sea, like rays from cold suns; icebergs rotted delicately in the spectra of midnight. Seaward over the archipelagoes moved never boat, never man, never shadow—only sometimes an eagle with whitened head and tail specking the late-lying snowfield upon one of ten thousand alps.

The eighth day out we anchored off Kayak Island to land and ship passengers. A black-haired, square-featured Apollo came aboard. He knew me. We had camped together a single night three years before on Copper River. I did not remember. Soon King told him how on a certain creek which the Government party had crossed a week out from Tyonek, Brooks had prospected 12½ cents to the pan, which meant wealth illimitable, if true. When we asked him to come with us, he said, "I'll make the trip with you to shake a pan in that crick—and to go with you." And the next morning, after we had left the town of Valdez in its ice-hung fjord, he looked at me and said, "Shanghaied!"

This was Jack, Scotch-Irish, and twenty-five. He had begun life as a breaker-boy in Pennsylvania collieries. His partner had died in his arms in the terrible winter of '98, starving and lost on Copper River. Jack was that immutable being, a prospector.

In two days we had entered Cook Inlet. Still we siphoned water for the thirsty horses, balancing buckets down ladders, as the mare we had named Bosco kicked herself crazy when you went near. At last we sighted the steam of the Redoubt volcano pouring over the snowy Chigmit range, and hove to one midnight, swinging the lead off Tyonek, on the west shore of the inlet, near its head.

CHAPTER IV

THE CAYUSE GAME

JUNE 23.—At three this morning we anchored a quarter mile off Tyonek, as the Swede sailors growled over the rail that the muddy tide was running eight miles an hour, though I rated it at four. Every one was sullen. Ashore, the low gables of the log store, weathered a pasty white, edged the beach; wolf-dogs whined beyond, crooked ridge-poles and ragged eaves hid Siwashes, and a terrace quilted with green gardens shot upward to the waste.

King showed up on deck, glum; then the Professor, who yawned: "Dunn, I think I shall disembark you first, to procure us a boat and a cabin." You see, we may send part of the outfit up Sushitna River in a boat, which the pack train can meet at the head of navigation, having traveled light over the first hundred miles of swamp. So the skipper rowed me ashore, and I woke Holt, the trader, a gaunt, Yankee-like man, who has boats galore.

The winch out on board began to squeak, lifting our horses from the hold—a band around their bellies, their legs pointed in, as you handle kittens—and dropped them one by one into the tide. The mate wouldn't bring his ship nearer shore, fearing to strand. The

Light Gray struck out into the Inlet, and was washed to the beach half a mile below town, squirting water from her nose. Then a boat-crew, holding each horse's tie-rope, caught them as they dived, led them in bucking the tide. It makes your heart jump, for not a beast seems to have a fighting chance, champing upright against the rip, grunting in terror till he reels from the icy water, forlorn and draggled. You can't help, for though it couldn't replace a horse, the steamer company is pledged to land all safely. I piloted about a Siwash boy tied to the Big Gray, as a mark for the swimmers, and between bites of Holt's fried mush and salmon, cursed the sailors for quitting a few beasts before they felt bottom. Sometimes one towed away a boat, or a tie-rope was dropped as we yelled; but all reached land, and I was sore that this swimming game turned out easier than we'd feared. Only the Light Gray was in bad shape. I rubbed her down with hay, and covered her with a blanket from a Swede fisherman's bunk in the deserted cabin we all share.

Then I was off to a native village five miles down the Inlet, where the crazy mare Bosco had led four of the bunch. A lonely, hot walk; but returning, I took along two Siwash kids to bully into herding the horses. And granite bowlders from the glacier that once filled the Inlet lay stranded like Titanic goose-eggs on glistening beds of rubbery wood-coal—and the Future, too, bewildered me. Back at Holt's, no one had landed. I sat on the board walk before the cabins till it was wet by the thirty-foot tide. Rank weeds squeezed through the planks; the terrace behind was purple with lupine, and tender birch leaves frittered in the wind. Along the squdgy tidal creek, gutted red salmon hung from cross-poles by Siwash huts in the long salt grass. Starved dogs, half-naked children, shawled klootches, bucks in prospectors' old clothes, all gathered, stared, shook hands, clucked questions. Home at last, in Alaska!

The rest of us landed, and broncho-busting began after a salmon dinner, cooked on the beach with lignite over the Professor's iron grid, which weighs a ton. First, we played Daniels, the den of horses being the log corral built long ago by the Government. We dodged heels and fangs, till we caught all the beasts. Through chinks in the logs we let out their neck-ropes, time and again to be kicked into snarls. When at last we had each horse tied separately outside, King applied nooses to their jaws, while we formed guys to the three cables on every broncho; tumbled and sprawled as they fought, till the hemp drew blood from their tongues, and, weary of bucking, they fell over backwards. Finally, each kneeled down as if to pray, which is the sign of surrender, and gingerly we clapped on hobbles, laughing as they took their first kangaroo steps.

Next—Bosco again. She had jumped the corral, and scooted to the wooded draws and benches of the terrace. For three hours, and as many miles south, west, and north, we scoured the devil's club for her, mosquito clouds a-roaring about our green head nets. And in vain....

It is ten o'clock at night. Jack and I have built a smudge on the beach. We sit watching the low East Foreland on the far shore of the Inlet, lying like a finger on the swirling water, which mirage dissolves and twists into watery dots and lines; now a dome, now a helmet, now a gourd. In the south glitters an endless, ghostly panorama of ice. At its heart, the broken cone of the Redoubt volcano (12,000 feet) trails dusky vapors from a column of pale steam, against a sky too pure for Heaven. And it seems the sun will never touch the horizon, and the heat of Sahara must beat forever on this land of snow and sunshine.

Jack says that the Swede fishermen nearly shot me for swiping that blanket.

JUNE 24.—Bronchos have tough gums and short memories. Life has become dodging horse heels, then hunting them.

To-day we played Daniels all over again. Still we noosed teeth. Still anchored to tie-ropes, each buck tumbled or lifted us in air, till a pack-saddle or two could slyly be slid over the gentler haunches. Early in the game, Simon slunk away to pack his duffle; next, the

Professor welched to fuss with his instruments. King and Jack didn't like that. They dropped remarks about people being "no good," and "afraid of work."

I knotted all the cinches, and rigged the saddle sling-ropes. We sacked the grub in fifty-pound canvas bags, and after hours of throwing diamond hitches, often a dozen times on the same beast, took a volcanic trial run up the beach; gathered in the scattered sacks; re-started the circus.

Then off to the outlaw Bosco, the only beast that has specified itself in our kicking nimbus of cayuse. I saw her through my cloud of pests on a windy angle of the terrace. Up went her tail like an inky fountain, and she snorted from half a mile off. On we struggled among the lakes, ridges, muskegs of the devil's club jungle. Even the Professor hunted. By afternoon we found the mashed grass where she slept last night and rolled off the flies. Just so did we yesterday; just so shall we to-morrow, in this country where they told us at Seldovia no white men will go in summer, fearing to be killed by the 'skeets.

Once, across a lake, a snow mountain rose over that maddening forest, a capless dome between smooth, wide shoulders—McKinley, by the gods! though two hundred miles away. Thus I got bearings and hit out for salt water, and in an hour slid down to high tide. Lucky, since I'd been lost a long time, with all Alaska to wander in. That's horse-hunting, in flat country, without a compass, and the sun circling drunkenly through the sky.

Jack has been talking with me, and not pleasantly. I don't want to write all he says—yet. He is dissatisfied, and offered to quit us. He doesn't like Simon or the Professor, because he doesn't understand tenderfeet. He has lived too long in Alaska. A man must go back to the States at least once in five years to keep sane. But this doesn't worry me, though Jack incites King to growl. They have become very intimate, sleep together, and are whispering there by the smudge as I write. Somehow I like Jack. I can't help it.

Four ruminative old trappers camped in a tent have been catching trout in the creek. They say that we can't pull out till tomorrow afternoon, when the tide is low, as the flood covers the beach up which we shall start to the head of the Inlet. The Professor suggests giving up Bosco, and King says it will take days, anyhow, to break her; yet I hate to have her best us.

Mount Iliamna and the snowy Chigmits over the West Foreland glow like molten copper. I am picking devil's club prickers out of my fingers before the poison suppurates. My enemies, the Swedes, who fish for the Kussiloff cannery down the Inlet, are carrying nets into their boats and soon will drift up-shore with the night tide. Neither clocks nor the sun rule life here; only the tide, the tide, filling, emptying this trough in the magic wilderness.

Jack says, "Note the mosquitoes have got their introduction, all right." Yes, they're biting like ——.

JUNE 25.—Here we're camped under the sea-terrace, in long sand grass, vetches, and driftwood, eight miles above Tyonek. Only the fat State o' Maine squawman saw us pull out toward afternoon; it seemed not to interest Holt or the trappers at all. We threw away the grid, and gave up Bosco to be bitten to death, for revenge. Packing took only four hours and we had no circus at the get-a-way. Not a beast bucked; the train only broke through a log-pile; the Professor, who led with the Big Bay on a long rope, was stood on his head, and Jack was tumbled for a foot-long hole in his overalls. We straggled north up the beach, Jack and I falling behind to smell for oil seepage in the sandy cliffs. At a ruined cannery the horses waded to their packs, and staggered out through quicksands.

Sure it's the first night on the long trail! I hear the first pot of Bayo beans a-bubbling, and the first dose of dried peaches is cold and porridgy by the lignite fire. Jack has burnt the beans, for such coal fire is hotter than you think. The Professor is taking a bath. Simon is mussing around, doing amusing, superfluous things with smudge fires, a whetstone and a brand-new knife, asking geometrical conundrums, and whittling a puzzle. Jack, stretched flat on his stomach, a red handkerchief over his head, is deep in my geology book. King is biting off chewing plug—in quarts. The fourteen horses are slowly back-trailing down the beach, stretching their necks for bunch-grass on the terrace.

Miller left Tyonek to-night on the rising tide with a third of the outfit in Holt's long, dory-like river boat. He is to follow up the shore and meet us to-morrow at the mouth of Beluga River; thence with Simon or the Professor to pole and cordel up Sushitna River, its west fork, the Skwentna, and that river's tributary, the Yentna. Roughly, the boat is to travel two sides of a right triangle, while we, hitting inland northwest, follow its hundred-mile hypotenuse, for the first fifty miles by a half-effaced winter trail. The land stretch, according to King, is too soft for horses packed with more than a hundred pounds each, and we must have a boat to ferry the grub at the Yentna and Skwentna fords.

Far across the Inlet, the snow-blue mountains, where Knick Arm breaks the range, open like mighty jaws. South rages the muddy tide out of the Inlet, bearing derelict cottonwoods on its bosom, which now and then we start up to gaze at, for their black roots seem to be swimming moose or bear.

Jack and I have lost our pipes. Wonderful, isn't it?—the æsthetic new oaths this country can inspire.

JUNE 26.—An hour to herd the horses over beach and terrace; another to make corrals with cinch ropes, noose their necks, tie each to a willow bush, unsnarl ropes and twigs, coax them one by one to the saddle and grub pile; more hours to blanket, saddle, sling packs and cinch. I'm up first about five, cooking. Jack and King hunt the beasts while I wash dishes and pack the white grub horse with the two panniers—'alforguses,' King calls them, which is Montanese for 'alforhaja'—that hold the pots and food we're using. Jack and I saddle and cinch seven horses; King and Simon seven. The Professor fusses about. He's very funny and energetic trying to catch the beasts.

Miller arrived unexpectedly on the tide at dawn and took Simon into the boat for the mouth of Beluga River, which we hit for overland, trailing inland from the beach.

Right by camp, the wild Dark Buckskin rolled down the bench, and chawed blood from my fingers when I dragged him up. Twice he fell into a crick, wedged on his back between logs, waving his legs, so we had to cut the tie-rope. The Professor looked on with a queer, quiet look. This is his first dose of cayusing in the North. Fred led the train with the Big Bay, we driving all in line, each behind his own four or five beasts. Even had we enough horses, it would be impossible for any one to ride. Too much doing.

We cursed and stumbled through snags and muck; staggered across open tundra; hacked the dense alders of treacherous cricks; halted to re-cinch one horse, while thirteen stampeded, wedging packs between the spruces. It was the familiar old game. Off bucks the Light Buckskin, his fifty-pound flour sacks spraying half an acre. Chase him, catch him, hunt the sacks, lug them up, re-saddle, re-cinch—while again the train wanders away, scraping off its load. Good Gawd! Then you must think of other lands and other sufferings. Hold your tongue, and see only the bursting rosebuds, the golden arnica, smell the sweet Labrador tea mashed by the floundering horses, behold the smooth benches of black loam and long red-top grass, and wonder why long ago Alaska was not settled, civilized, and spoiled. Why, to-day I saw lots of old stumps starry-white with bunch-berry flowers, as if cultivated there!

The Professor took things stolidly. I think he would face death and disaster without a word, but through the insensitiveness of age and too much experience, rather than by true courage. I cannot believe he has imagination; of a leader's qualities he has shown not one. He seems our sympathetic servant. I suspect no iron hand be-

hind his innocence. He doesn't smoke, and that makes me uncom-
fortable....

At two o'clock we reached this grassy alder swamp, each in his
'skeet cloud-of-witnesses, where the terrace dips down to the
melancholy tide-flats of the Beluga, strewn with wrecked spruces.
Belugas, which are white whales, were plunging shoulders in the
river, as should be. A white fan emerges from water the color of
café au lait, with a "tsschussk," as if it belched steam. And an old
brown bear, pawing for candle-fish, looked at us in a lazy, human
way, and galumphed off slowly into the cottonwoods across the
sticky silt.

Simon and Miller came in with the boat at eight o'clock. I doubted
if they'd make it. If they hadn't, they couldn't take the boat to the
Skwentna ford, and have no business on this trip. That's all.

Jack and I have unloaded the boat, and ferried everything that the
pack train is to carry to the north side of the river. Again and again
we crossed the brown swirl, till even when we looked at them from
shore the very woods still swam inland. We pulled off our arms
bucking the current straight, hitting land half a mile below our aim
and cordeling up. The thirty-foot tide was rising, but under the current, which it simply lifts without slacking. Then, like nigger coal-
heavers in the tropics, we hustled the sacks on our backs from shore
into the bear's cottonwoods, wallowing ankle-deep in the glacial
muck. The 'skeets, as always in such desperate work, enraged us.

Jack and I are alone on the far side of the river. It is raining; we
have no tent, and I am trying to make the small sleeping-bag water-
proof and mosquito-proof with a poncho and a head-net. It's no
use. We'll fight them awake and sopping to-night.

I wonder what's going to happen to us these next three months.
Everything's easy so far....

We're over here, you see, to shoo Mr. Bear from the bacon.

CHAPTER V

THE FORBIDDEN TUNDRA

JUNE 27.—First, we swam the horses across the Beluga. It's no worse than landing them from a ship, except as risking a basket of eggs is worse than risking eggs singly. We hand-corraled them with cinches on shore at low tide, when we thought they couldn't jump back up the bank, not because the current lessens—it never does. But up the bank they dashed through the ropes, and a dozen times we fought them back through the alders. With all inside the rope at last, King and I swept them into the river with it, like minnows in a net, the others shouting and stoning. They hesitate. Plunge. The current wiggles them as they stand upright at first, churning the water with their fore hoofs; strews them out in irregular parabolas toward the far shore, some swimming madly, and as they weaken, drifting down; others calmly, at last reaching up-stream or colliding with the weaker ones. Then the tightness in your heart relaxes, for they all snort in chorus, and it bewilders you to see them struggle up the slimy bank, one by one, scattered out for half a mile.

Till noon we were packing them with the solid fifty-pound sacks—flour, bacon, beans, two bags to each horse—and loading the boat with the mountain-climbing outfit, instrument boxes and all unwieldy stuff. The Professor suddenly decided offhand, consulting no one, to take the river trip with Miller alone. So Simon is with us. We didn't want him, and King tried to make me hint a protest to the Professor, but I wouldn't. So I'm in charge of the main outfit, for ten days at least, through what's said to be the wettest, most desperate mushing in Alaska; responsible for three men I never knew a month ago: a little New York Jew, a young sourdough, and a Montana packer who was with Brooks of the Geological Survey when he crossed this stretch. He (King) says that the Indian trail we follow runs about west into the foot-hills of the Tordrillo Mountains; then is lost, and we must hit due north to Skwentna River.

"Dunn," said the Professor, as we parted, "under average conditions it is to be expected that we shall meet at the Skwentna ford in rather more than eight days." I hope so. Anyhow, new trails open in the old wilderness of life....

Later, and God knows where. The real thing just hit us. This winter trail we follow led from the birchy Beluga straight out into tundra, through line after line of ratty spruces, where you sink ankle-deep into sick, yellow moss, and wobbly little ridges separate small ponds. Suddenly every horse was down, kicking and grunting helplessly in the mud. They lost their heads. They seemed to like to jump off into the ponds. We tugged, hauled, kicked at the brutes; unpacked the sacks, lugged them to shore, pulled on tie-ropes, tails; batted heads, poured water down nostrils till they hissed like serpents. One was out, another was down. Oh, our beautiful oaths! Hot, hungry, dizzy, insane with mosquitoes, we struggled waist-deep in yellow muck, unsnarling slimy cinches, packing, repacking the shivering, exhausted beasts. It was endless. Torture.

We kept to dry gullies toward the river-bed, we kept to tundra; but always the train tore through the iron-fingered scrub spruce, ripping packs, snagging hoofs, tumbling us at the end of lead lines.

Mount Sushitna tormented us, floating, patched with snow over the sickish forest; and the long, low hill we're aimin' for, laid out in green squares of tropic grass and alders, seemed forever to recede. I call it Alice's Hill, after "Through the Looking Glass." Remember her perverse garden.

Jack went off at half-cock. "Just the sort of a —— trail a —— old woman like that —— Brooks would follow," he yelled; and when I said this was a pretty hard deal, the first crack out of the box, he shouted: "What yer blamin' King for? It ain't his fault."

All had been down for the tenth time, and a horse can't stand much more. Some one said "Camp." We'd gone only four miles; it was six o'clock. Fred looked at me. "It's up to you, you're the Professor," he drawled. Responsibility bit.

So we've camped. No grass for the horses; mud water, and yet Fred, who moves so calmly and surely when all seems down and lost, who isn't supposed to touch a frypan, has volunteered to bake the bread. Wonderful man—or is it he thinks I can't?

I've put a cheese-cloth door in the tent,—oh, just to whet the 'skeet appetites. Jack is snoring, exhausted. The horse blankets we try to sleep in—we've nothing else, the Professor swiped the sleeping-bags—are soaked. Good-night.

JUNE 28.—Two days' travel, and we've gone eight miles! At this rate we won't see McKinley till winter.

Calvin, when he manufactured his own hand-made hell, must have been to Alaska. Oh, yes, King says that last year the ground had not thawed out here as much as this. But, by Heaven, we'll make it!

Yesterday was only a hint; watering the brutes' nostrils was child's play to how we kicked their necks and eyes to-day; being dragged and snagged through the scrub was fun to how we've been hunting Alaska over just now for shipped packs, to how we'd meet a pond after a mile-long detour, and have to track back again with the same antics.

The old White, Big Buckskin, who is much too aged and heavy for this game, the Bay Mare carrying our dunnage, would all flounder *together* into each pond. Still Alice's Hill, and Mount Sushitna, north at the head of the Inlet, mocked us. Still the sickish, tufted spruces dwarfed one another in plague-stricken procession down into the stinking yellow sphagnum of these hot ponds. We fished the soaked food sacks out from the little white flowers floating on top. Sank to our knees at every step, seeming to lift a ton on each boot.

Hot, hungry, dizzy, we fell into camp by this grassy stream. I kept on alone over the mile-long tundra beyond it, to see the worst ahead for to-morrow. Responsibility was not wearing me. If we don't get through, it will be no fault of ours. Glossy snows cloaked Mount Spurr (11,000 feet) in the southwest. I floundered across a backbone of red moss, climbed its lower slopes twice, to more tundra and fearful mud holes. This damned winter trail! You can't write the thoughts you have alone on the tundra, dragging onward three men by a trail leading from nowhere to nowhere, where we shall never pass a soul nor see sign of man for months. Sand-hill cranes with scarlet wings and red heads floated away, with squawks like wood-wedged axes. Twice I sank to rest in the moss, and found I was crawling on. I tried to smoke, but it only sickened me....

But now I have eaten—*eaten*—six enormous bannocks, six plates of Bayo beans, four cups of tea like lye, and I feel better than I have ever felt, in any state of intoxication, by anything. Alaska proves the law of compensation. I have just shaved, with the tin reflector which bakes the bread for a mirror. King is spreading Simon's mosquito goo on his face, just to prove it's no good. Simon, who has catarrh, is snuffing things up his nose from a crooked glass tube. Jack is telling how once he cleaned up a temperance hotel....

JUNE 29.—Over Alice's Hill!

I started out dead tired. I'd never suffered from real exhaustion before. You can't write much these days.

Let any one make any comment on the trail, and Jack turns it into a personal insult. He's just hurled away the axe, while chopping fire wood, as if it had bitten or spoken to him.

When the Dark Buckskin, the meanest horse in the bunch, jumped into a pond for the third time to-day, and I after, to haul him out, I splashed Jack, and he cursed me for five minutes. He's Irish, so it doesn't mean much. Later I apologized. He gaped. I saw it "took." To manage him you must be polite, oh, so very polite, and do little favors for him when he doesn't expect them; for he does work like fury, and thinks no one else can. Simon said on the trail to-day that Jack wouldn't stick with us, "because he's Irish." "Think so?" said I, nastily, remembering what Simon is. After all, with us four, the leadership is coming down to a tussle between Jack and me. He has more power, but I hope I have intelligence and—forbearance. When he attacks me, I can only say, "I can't argue the matter."

The hill made only a short break in the floundering ponds and steely scrub. Tundra still succeeded tundra. You think you're at the end of all, pass through a slim line of spruces, a birch or two, a yard of dry ground—out again upon another tundra. It makes you dizzy.

Simon is absolutely dazed; has real old Alaska numbness; can't move, or think, or hear. He doesn't even know how to cook, nor seem to want to learn. He has absolutely no initiative, which I suppose is racial. But I pity him. Nine men out of ten fresh from the city wouldn't do half as well—couldn't stand this. Yet once to-day I heard him singing his college song; and Jack, after cursing the Professor, Simon, King, and every one, bursts into a magnificent whistle of "The Wearing of the Green," looks at me, and grins. We're sure a great outfit, all properly a little wary of one another. I don't know whether I boss too much or not enough. I don't give many orders, surely.

Thus we still hit west, toward the foot-hills of the Tordrillo range, though the Skwentna ford is northwest.

Thus the day ended in a kind of daze. The beasts shivering, packs dripping mud, we came out on a grassy terrace over a red little stream. "No horses ken stand more 'n a day more of this traveling," said King. And no one gave the order to unpack....

The reason this Diary seems so good-humored, is because it's always written *after* eating. Never write a field journal on an empty stomach. You'll hate yourself, if you do, when you read it over after eating. Every word of this is second thought, well considered and digested, with a day's good hard work done behind it.

We've swallowed boiled rice with milk—which must be used up, as the cans are splitting open—reflector-bread, and tea.

Brushed my teeth to-night.

JUNE 30.—Guess I was near insane this morning, up first by an hour, as usual, boiling rice. Yes, from gnats; millions of them besides the 'skeets and so small you can't see them burrowing into your skin. Then came whiffs of breeze, and the sun shone yellow. Forest fires, somewhere, thank Heaven! smoke scattering the midges.

We packed in only four hours. Still we crossed tundra, but the ponds were drier. Hardly a horse went down, hardly a pack slipped. In the west, the Tordrillo Mountains glittered through the smoke like blue glass inlaid with ivory, Mount Spurr floating over all like a shadowy cap of Liberty. Land here from a balloon, and you would think this Hades Eden: green lawns of six-foot red-top border the tundra, with here and there a drooping birch, and scattered spruces, slimmer and more delicate than I've ever seen. You expect to see country villas, glassed piazzas, red chimneys—and there is nothing, nothing. It is very weird; often it's terrible.

To-night we're in the tent on a lush grass slope by the eternal swamp. Sometimes it's up with the tent, sometimes not; all depends on the 'skeets. Jack has been washing his feet. "Put down it's for the first time," he tells me, seeing me writing. (I haven't washed mine at all yet.) Simon is mending his drawers, and King has been telling a diverting tale about a Christmas dance at Big Hole, Montana. I've been sitting over the crick, cutting the hairs off my chafed legs with the water for a mirror. Thus I spilt the beans just put there to soak. Last night we forgot to soak them, so every one had gripes from bean-poisoning....

The extra-condemned, in the extra-wet, innermost circle of the Inferno, should be whipped on to mush forever in these boots the Professor has given us. Oh, no, this inch-soled green leather won't harden—that's supposed to be its great virtue; how could it in this floating-island country? My uppers are ripped to rags by snags, and the nails have all dropped out—just like the new-fangled stuff of a New York "sporting" outfitter.

JULY 1.—Under the Tordrillo foot-hills.

We lost the winter trail for good to-day, so I had to choose between routes: to reach the Skwentna traveling west two days more, then north along the foot-hills; or by going down a big north-flowing stream, the Talushalitna (we suppose) which we crossed at noon, and must meet the Skwentna. The Professor encouraged me once when I suggested following it. But the hills beckoned for two reasons, the river for only one—shorter air-line distance, which means nothing in this country, where the shortest trail is the easiest, not the least in miles. Hitting down the stream would mean two days' steady going where gouged banks showed we'd have to swing from shore to shore, besides losing a day in chopping trail ahead through dense alders and a swampier country yet, for every day traveled. Going around by the hills, first, no trail need be cut, and we should reach the ford in five days by a dry route King has been over. Second, and most important, we should pass the fabled crick where, he said, Brooks had prospected 12½ cents gold to the pan—which means wealth untold though it doesn't sound so—to find which had partly brought Jack with us. Jack gets no pay, and I've never seen a man work harder, even if he does lose his temper.

We have hit for the hills. I decided quickly, ready to repent, but haven't yet. I'm sick of these swamps and ponds. Simon kicked, saying I wasn't facing my issues squarely. "If you want to prospect, say so," he growled. That's his selfishness. He'd attract a man to a God-forsaken country on a wild gold tale, and then conveniently forget it. "You'd face issues more squarely if you'd learn to be useful about camp," I said. Once I told the Professor that Simon was generally inefficient. He said, "Teach him to cook." Did I come to Alaska to start a cook-and-camping school? I told Simon to follow or not, as he chose.

Right off he did a pretty thing. Dashes away with his ladies' .22 rifle, lets the horses he's driving go to hellangone, and pops twenty times at a mud hen in a puddle ten yards off. Half an hour later, I see blood on the grass; then Jack shows me Big Buck's cheek dripping red. At first we thought it snagged, but the hole was small, and through the bone. Simon had shot him. "Alasky is no place fer little boys with girls' guns," observed Fred.

We're camped by a large clear stream, with mossy springs along the bank, and wide willow flats below. The brutes are eating their heads off in bunch-grass, which is the best sort. Big Buck has wiped the blood from his face, and is lying down. Hope to Heaven he won't get poisoned, as we've no antiseptic along. King says it's useless to wash the hole—yet; and he knows best about such things.

"I'd like ter see the old Professor a-draggin' his behind off acrost these swamps," he's just drawled. Yes, I'd like to see any scientific observer of icebergs from the deck of a plush-converted exploring whaler fighting bronchos and 'skeets in this Alaskan muck. Funnier than the Sunday-school tale he'd write about it. I'd stake any drunken Valdez musher against such.

As for King; the frankness of the Rocky mountaineer is the best fairy tale I know. He's always hiding what he really thinks about the trail and outfit while preaching the abstract laws of existence. You can't keep him to an argument, nor tell him anything, except about your limited civilized sphere, at which he gapes and changes the subject. Here's a typical thing. Two days ago, I heard Fred and Jack indulging in the favorite Alaskan pastime of "cussing the country"— some Sitka official in particular who said it would support farms. "It's too hard for Swedes," they said, and Swedes aren't considered white men up here. Now traveling's better, I'm hearing them say that Alaska's the only God's country, and they're coming here some day to ranch cattle! But I love them all. Sometimes I think I'm too childishly confidential, but can you be too intimate with your fellows in this soul-scarring game? You can't, and I'll stick it out so to the end, though to-day when I asked Jack and Fred to call me by my first name they seemed to shy....

This is a long, pointless drool for a poor musher in this wet Hades, but we've made two o'clock camp. I've got the fruit and beans a-boiling, shaken a gold pan in the stream, monkeyed with the map and compass for a guess where on the face of the earth we are, and taken a bath. Now I must water the beans, and put in the pot the old pieces of bacon we don't eat and keep in the aluminum grease cup. We haven't been able to carry cooked beans, and at the half-hour noon halt have eaten from our pockets, bread I cook in the reflector after washing dishes and before packing every morning. But to-morrow we're going to put cooked beans in Simon's botanizing tin. Also, it will keep him from delaying the train by picking up flowers by the roots along the trail.

JULY 2.—In the Tordrillo foot-hills.

Thunder last night brought all-day rain. Lighting the breakfast fire, I found that the Professor had sent us off with about a dozen matches, so Simon fired his girl's .22 into his botany-collector's paper for a blaze. Nothing's nastier than breaking a wet camp, pulling on tough, soggy cinches, knowing that the wet leaks into the precious grub through the pack-covers where the ropes bind. Only worse is traveling in the wet.

At a big lake we waded exactly thirty-four tributary streams. Then up, up we hit into the hills in dense fog, guessing at directions. Copses of dense alders dotted the rank grass with even, artful luxuriance. Snow-beds shrinking in the gullies on dead, flattened grass, were edged by white flowers with waxy green leaves. Black cliffs sprang overhead. Forever we toiled blindly over glacier-rounded ridges, now snow-covered and pink with *nivalis,* now tropically clad—I, fool that I was, shivering through the drizzle in only a sweater and overalls.

Once Simon let his horses stampede past a cut bank over a stream down which Fred had cut trail. Jack was so mad he lunged out with his stick and batted the little Baldface into the alders down the slope, so he rolled over on his back, cutting a swath; a goner, thought I. I swam the stream, fighting through the brush to head off the bunch and get axes to chop him out. When free, he limped— but, Lord! you can't write the pity and desperation of such stunts.

Curving north, again we mounted to the sky, lost in clouds and among mud-holes, tiny dried ponds, great bowlders, and beds of Labrador tea. Late, we struck down from under the fog; and there, beneath the azure cloud-edge, glimmered again the flat swamp country. "Timber!" we shouted together. I made a fool of myself by mislaying the axes as we counseled which distant saddle ahead to cross; and we floundered down through alders to a lush grass meadow, a melting snow-bank, and four spruce trees.

Over a huge, burning stump we have loaded cinch ropes with socks, drawers and overalls. Dunnage, grub, everything, is soaked. The tea, rice, and sugar sacks are propped before the fire; the beans, fruit and flour, which wet hurts less, are cached under the tiny spruce trees, each pair of sacks with its saddle. Fruit only mildews, and flour forms a wet layer just inside the canvas, which dries hard as a rock, and waterproof.

Simon is still eating, throwing away the insides of my biscuit. He complains they won't digest. "Lots of weaknesses a man don't suspect he has, show up in this country," observes Fred. "Too much botany's the trouble with him," growls Jack, "and I've noted it to that effect." No one's good-humored.

All to-day rhymes buzzed in my head. This one hardest, which I can't locate:

> Let me feel maggots crawling in the sod,
> Or else—Let me be God!

Just now, "Hist! said Kate the Queen," is the line bothering me, which I think is Browning. All this may be very foolish, but many things called foolish at home seem right sensible up here. Anyway, most things that seem sensible at home appear foolish up here. Big Buck isn't poisoned yet, which is sound, however you take it.

CHAPTER VI

The Vanishing Ford

July 3.—Not a wink, sleeping by the burning stump. Its heat drew the 'skeets, and the old punk blazed up like a blast-furnace, nearly finishing my horse-blankets.

Packed at last, and with the sun shining, we jumped right into rotten luck. At a big stream, the brown horse branded B refused to take the trail we'd cut through the alder jungle, and jumped in up to his neck—three times. Once, four beasts together followed him, wetting their packs, too, carried downstream and mixed up in snags and swift water, till the game seemed up. Twice I plunged in to my eyes and soaked my camera. Jack and I sweated like crazy men, and only King came back to help. No sooner were the four on the trail, than we hit a sheer alder slope, and chopped upward. It was too steep for the poor Whiteface, who staggered over backwards and rolled to the bottom, caught on his back in the vicious stems. When roped out, repacked, and hauled up the bank, both hind legs limped. His back can't stand much more.

At last we crossed the 12½ cent crick. The 'skeets were so thick, Jack lost his temper, hurled away the gold-pan, and vented his wrath on Simon, simply because the boy stood near, with the .22 gun in his hand, watching. When King called something from a distance, Jack yelled back, "I don't want no *hee* nor *haw* from you, neither!" We left him to track us to camp; struck better going, crossing another divide by two small ponds under toothed, snowy mountains cut by vast amphitheatres.

Then came King's turn. We sighted an old she-grizzly, humping up a slope with two cubs swinging after. Out Fred whips his rifle and snaps the magazine. The cartridges won't fit the barrel. He jams them and swears; studies them. They're .303 Savage all right, which the gun should be. Mrs. Bear lifts her fat rear over the hill, laughing a good bear laugh, I guess. Fred looks at the barrel. It's a .30-30 Winchester! If the Seattle gun-store clerk that palmed off that rifle on us had been within fifty miles, he'd have thought quick about his life insurance. Of course it was our fault. We bought a Savage, handed it to the clerk to put on peep sights, which he put on another gun, handing it back to us next day; and we neglected to examine before freighting it. Yet, right now that clerk's life, were he here in Alaska, wouldn't be worth that old she-bear's laugh.

Here in camp, we're baking in the reflector with a green willow fire, which is like running a steam engine by burning matches under the boiler. Simon, who has been off after ptarmigan, comes back with a mess of green fern-tops that he wants to eat to tune up his insides, and is asking us how to cook them. Jack returns furious with the 'skeets, and "whoever lied about the gold in that crick." He panned just four colors. Thus we sit and discuss how big the Talushalitna River must be where it meets the Skwentna; how this gravel wash got among these volcanic mountains....

We're going to bed. Jack is to sleep next to the tent door to try and keep the 'skeets out, for every one else has failed. Simon will soon suspend from the cheese-cloth, fake mosquito-proof door, his spectacles and watch—our only one. He will forget to wind the watch. But he is long-suffering and kicks at nothing. Yet I prefer volatile men like Jack to the easy-going sort. I'd rather see a man vent at God and Nature the wrath you can't help feeling in this country, by breaking loose and ripping things up now and then, rather than swallow it all mutely. The Simon sort don't feel the wrath; haven't the sensitiveness. They don't forbear. But which travels furthest, and, reaching his end, gets the keenest joy? Yet, not he who has forborne.

The horse-bell has the mosquito-jumps. This bending over pots and panniers makes my back ache. Hands are so dirty you could plant potatoes in their creases.

July 4.—'Skeets drove the horses back two miles beyond the little lakes, and we weren't packed till eleven. Traveling was bully, all high up over snowfields and meadows. Three hours, and the Skwentna glittered far below, a dim flashing network of bars and thready channels. Mountain range after range glimmered blue and snowy through the haze beyond. We sat to gaze, eating four biscuits apiece from my mackinaw pocket, washed down with water from a snow-puddle. Said Simon, "I've decided you can't hunt birds and drive pack horses at the same time." We sighed. At last! But in this resolve there's no repentance for leaving the horses he drives to wander off and slip packs, while he waddles after ptarmigan that he's too blind to see, and couldn't hit even if he wasn't. Simply because we went so fast to-day it winded him awfully, chasing up a hill to catch us!

We mounted a rock peak, and chopped an endless way through alder jungles to a meadow by a gorged stream. Here we're camped. The sorrel branded P.R., stampeding down through the scrub, shipped the unwieldly box Simon keeps his roots in. A box has no business on a pack horse, anyway, and I felt like leaving it in the muck, which wouldn't be loyal; so back I plugged a mile, and repacked it for the kid....

I'm shaving in the reflector. The P.R. Sorrel has kicked King's right ankle black and blue, and I have wrapped it with electric tape. Simon has produced from his dunnage a mashed box of wet candy, and is doling us out pieces, one by one. Says he's going to save some for his birthday. Now, instead of chucking away the biscuit insides, he has a way of frying them—monopolizing the fire and the pans as we need them for the common weal. Drat him! He won't believe it when we tell him fried bread's harder to digest than doughy. But he doesn't bother me much. I only wish he had more initiative. I suppose it's racial that he hasn't. The Jew has always been the selfish follower-on, the scavenger of civilization, just as we Yankees have been the bullying pioneers. Hobson's choice. One thing, Simon doesn't lose his temper, and I believe he'd stand a lot of pounding in this life.

JULY 5.—At the Skwentna!

The watch stopped in the night, and I guessed at five o'clock. We ate, packed, and plunged into the worst day yet, going hardly five miles.

Fred's ankle was very sore, and I offered to lay over. He wouldn't decide, and seemed ready to move. I asked Jack's advice. "No man could make me travel this country with a foot like that," he broke out, "but that's King's business." And King began packing.

By noon, it seemed that we'd been traveling a year, hewing down, down, stem by stem, among the iron-limbed alders. Winter snows flatten, toughen, bind, and bend them into tempered springs. You can't move an inch without an axe, or getting gouged in the face. And then to drive fourteen exhausted, half-wild bronchos, stampeding, snorting, as you hear the whooping-screeching rip of canvas—see the cinches dangling from the brush! Oh, our hot oaths as we hunt and gather the packs, chopping a clear space to pack, fighting mosquitoes! And for every foot the beasts travel we cover forty, dashing forward to head them, unsnarl, drag from the mud.

Simon hasn't the least control over his brutes. Just says "Git up!"

moves a fat leg slowly—and they're all fighting crazy off the trail. Once to-day the Roan rubbed off his pack, and I chased him back half the day's going. Simon simply waited by the load, without carrying it to the open for repacking. I slopped over for the first time on the trip. The horses he helped pack, I said, always slipped cinches first. "That's a lie!" he blazed out—"or at least you're mistaken." "Better make it 'mistaken,'" said I, and Jack grinned, as we hauled the cinch. King says I draw the cinches too tight—perhaps I do, thank God—and crowd the beasts on the trail.

We reached a big crick paralleling the river. The banks were slewed and clogged with drift and willows. We were an hour crossing and ploughing through the quicksands, finding the lead for trail beyond. Simon was swept off his feet fording it. He didn't seem in much danger, though the foam-collars on the rocks bowled him pretty hard, and before I could reach the water, Jack, who's been talking as if he'd like to kill the kid, jumped in and made a rescue. We crossed, each braced on a pole, and lost our feet only for a few yards. No man can stand more than waist-high in a glacier stream, so the runts suffer.

Cutting trail with me on the other side and piling brush to keep the beasts from jumping into the crick where it turned and gouged the bank, Jack suddenly lost his temper for no reason I could see, and hurled off his axe murderously into the brush. Then he snagged his eye, and sat down, quivering for ten minutes on the sand-bar, his head in his hands, so no one dared speak to him.

The river woods were rich and wonderful, and late we came out by the Swentna. Rose vines in full bloom, each with countless flowers of every scarlet hue, clung to tall spruces; immense dark violets and meads of anemones dotted the moss. Then opened below the mile-wide wilderness of the river's willow bars and sandy channels; came its low, metallic roar in the hot sunlight. We were nearly dead. The 'skeets were crazing us. The idiot skinny Bay ran amuck, and we were half an hour finding her pack and catching her. I suggested camp. Fred seemed to want to, but wouldn't suggest. I asked Jack. "I don't give my opinion no more," he shouted. "I give it once to-day, and no attention was paid to it." Thus we camped here....

King's ankle has turned blue, but hurts little in walking. Here in the tent, he's pining for the Fourth-o'-July dance at his home in Montana. "But I wouldn't be no good with this ankle," he drawls. Simon actually fetched glacier-water from the river for cooking supper without being told, but mired himself with the pots halfway up the bank, so I had to come to his rescue. Then he cooked a weird mess of fern-tops and dried-pea soup to discipline his insides. Now he's out cooking fruit—for another cure. Jack is putting tea-leaves on his sore eye, and reading the *Fortnightly Review* with the other. Our portable library contains "Pelham" (Bulwer-Lytton), "Ardath" (Marie C[orelli])—the Professor's favorite, "Tom Sawyer," mine, a magazine or two, and some funny books on the "Hints to Explorers" order. King, who is now asleep with his mouth open, and Simon, don't read. Feels like rain.

I marvel that Jack isn't more cut-up at not finding his Eldorado in that crick. Some one's made a mistake, but he bears no malice; accepts it as if he'd only lost a sock or half a dollar, willing to plug right along. It must always be thus with prospectors; each means to their vast ends ever fizzles out, ever becomes more insignificant as the great dream grows....

Fred says that he thinks from this camp Brooks traveled one day to the ford, going down the river; but his uncertainty worries me.

JULY 6.—The very devil of a day! Rain splashed the tent at daylight, and sourly we ate a soggy breakfast, though I had lit the fire on the first match—nearly our last. We hardly saw Brooks' track once, threading meadows, slews, ponds, steep scarps. One fiery 'skeet cloud hummed with us, and the sodden drip of rain washed their poison like sharp acid down our streaming necks and faces. Once we traveled three miles in a circle, coming out in the same old tundra; halted an hour to find the lead out of a meadow; struck the crick we crossed yesterday, and chawed on soaked biscuit. Into its snags and drift-piles we stoned the brutes, and Simon, jumping on the White Grub horse, was bucked off, *kersplash!*

Unsuspiciously we struck a meadow and a quiet stream, fording its countless arms through dense willows. Every horse went down, scrambling up an old beaver dam. Floundering on, I suddenly saw the water rising fast up their legs. So the big rats had just felled the last tree somewhere below to choke a new dam's opening! We were trapped. King and Jack ahead were hewing trail through willows. Into the pond I had to drive the horses; out we had to get like a flash, the shortest way. Each after each was mired, rolling about in the muck and rising water, clinging like spiders to the dam-edge. It was one of those fearful Alaskan moments, when you realize all may be lost at the give of a single horse-tendon—and you care, and don't give a damn, oh, so intensely! If I gave a hopeless look, as we beat and dragged and unpacked them, Fred shook his head, meaning perhaps it was all futile; but he worked so leisurely, that somehow we did get the train out with every ounce of grub soaked, sloshed through more ponds, climbed a bench to camp.

"Here's where Brooks stopped," said King, "and I guess he was two days more from here making the ford." A wonderful sense of locality and power to smell out the easiest way across bad country has he, but no visual memory, or power to tell you and act on half what he does know. I know we must cross the Talushalitna before meeting the Professor at the ford. Fred has said all along he believes that the ford is this side of the tributary, which he doesn't remember having crossed. Now this camp suddenly recalls everything—that we must cross the Talushalitna, that while fording it last year the Government horses wet their packs, that there's no horsefeed and so no camp near it!

We've built fires to dry the blankets, to sleep in, and because wet ones gall the beasts' backs. Jack and Fred are hunting a dry spruce to sleep under—it still rains—and Simon, fussing with the tent, is swearing beautifully.

Jack, who began life working in the Alleghany coal mines, afterward became a plumber, and is telling the secrets of that trade. Simon is drawing him out, giggling, and condescendingly repeating Jack's serious expressions as to the fight for existence he's been through, in the way I don't like. Fred takes up the tale with a Boccaccio-like adventure—Montana characters and local color.... (There's the climax.) I've wrapped my feet up in a mackinaw, folded the driest parts of horse-blankets in strips across my stomach, thus to sleep. We all get pains in our legs every night, for we never dry off—rheumatics, I guess.

JULY 7.—Anywhere.

And still no Skwentna ford. Of course, now we're wishing we'd gone down the Talushalitna, which still eludes us.

The rain stopped at dawn, and we made good time till we hit a swag where Fred said Brooks got lost last year. Sure, it's the best lose-yourself-country ever: flat in the large, with tag-ends of benches and ridges, all hurled together at right angles; one-pond swamps, timber, cup-like meadows with grass to your shoulder. At three o'clock, after eating beans poured from the botany tin out of my old bandana, we reached a longish lake with a gravelly bottom. "Yes, sir, and there's Brooks' next camp," pointed King across a slew. Confound such a memory!

So here by the lake, Fred has a big, yellow cow-lily stuck in his hair. Simon is mending his overalls with what Jack calls a base-ball stitch. Jack, in the red diary I gave him, is writing nasty things about all of us, I'm sure. And *no* mosquitoes!—though it's their field-hour, for rain threatens. Who'll ever write the Alaskan mosquitoad? Why, for instance, are the small, yellow ones commoner than the big black sons-o'-guns in these parts? When it blows hard, do they sink into the grass and sneak along after you, so the same ones attack when the gust's over, or does a new troop come out? Does the same thirsty cloud follow you for miles, or do the gratified gluttons drop back, kindly giving 'way to new empty-bellies? Where are they now? There's good fodder for scientific research, to benefit Alaskan mankind. And here's more: I saw two little yellow frogs in a swamp to-day, but held my tongue so Simon wouldn't harpoon them.

A pair of sneakers up here lasts just two days. I sleep in my Scotch homespuns, and have just learned to keep my pipe and to-bacco in their pockets daytimes, not to have to dry the plug each night by the fire in the large dough spoon. My overalls are worn through at the knees from puttering over cook-fires, and all my fin-gers are a quarter inch too thick and cracking at the joints....

We are telling stories and limericks. I'm going to sleep by Jack's private blanket-drying fire. Wonder where the Professor is, and if the 'skeets have chewed off his long hair.

CHAPTER VII

LAST STRAWS

JULY 8.—Sh-sh-sh!

In two hours we made a large clear stream between high diorite cliffs—the Talushalitna! Every time I leaped behind a horse's pack in fording it, a bunch of them tore back to shore; so I crossed alone on foot, through a hundred tickliest yards of icy water. Then we covered endless meadows and one-pond swamps, purple with iris, golden with arnica. Jack's horses stampeded, and he flew into a passion. Now we slid down grassy benches, to a silty slew, where the bent willows were rust-red with glacial mud—from river-floods! Glad omen! But never was reapproach to a river so vanishing: more sloughs and silt flats, a level spruce forest growing from white moss and roses; at last a lead along an endless, gouged drift-pile, and we heard shouts, and saw two tents on a gravel island in the middle of the brown river. The Professor, Miller, and two Siwashes, one big, one little, cavorted across to us in a long boat. Our leader first gravely shook my hand and smiled. "Hello, Dunn," said he (like that prig Stanley's icy, "Mr. Livingstone, I believe?" when he met the missionary in darkest Africa, thought I). "You've done excellently. We arrived here only this morning." Mosquito hats choked all of them. They blind and deafen, and if a man as God made him can't stand the 'skeets, he's no right up in this country.

We started to ford, from the south shore to the north. The Bay Dunnage mare was mired in a quicksand and pulled out before we even unpacked and loaded the boat. It was the best place ever for putting in horses to swim, a cut bank they couldn't climb up on their side, a narrow current nearly all in one channel and shooting across diagonally to the other shore, where a long bar stretched below. I crossed to the island—only a shallow channel's on the other side—to dry the wet grub at once, as the sugar is syruping away, and the bacon is green with mould. There I heard Jack and King stoning and shouting like maniacs, sweeping the bunch into the current with stretched cinches. Miller was popping his camera at them. At that instant the P.R. Sorrel, leading all in mid-stream, made back for shore! Snorting in spasms, the whole crew followed. The Professor and I dashed into the boat, and hit out to head them off. Jack tore down the south bank, yelling and rocking them like a crazy man. Three or four miraculously climbed out on his side, despite him and the cut bank. Again all depended on one fiber of one horse. We in the boat got below them on Jack's side, but they shot past, all headed with the current, straight for the snag-pile at the bend. That meant drowning for all—when one beast turned by some miracle, and seemed to lead all, grunting more and more faintly, to the tail end of the bar, saving them by ten yards!

So the whole train was scattered on both sides of the river. We counted them again and again, and made only ten out of the fourteen. We shouted and shouted from bank to bank. No use. We found the three that had scrambled up the bad bank, and Jack had an idea that the Light Gray had gone with them. But we sighted him on the north bank. So only one remained missing, and in vain we dragged the brush and back-trailed. At last Simon, who is always three days behind time, said he'd seen Dark Buck shooting straight down with the current around the drift pile, when the bunch had made for the bar. The Professor, Miller, and he, being on the island with the boat, pursued in it downstream. We swam the three beasts that had climbed the cut bank, standing waist deep in the quicksand, hurling rocks. They made the bar well; we crossed swimming, and gorged on oatmeal and potatoes; then drove the bunch from the island across the shallow channel, safe on the north side of the Skwentna, at last.

In an hour the Professor came back. "We've lost another horse," said he hopelessly—his face is growing white in this Alaskan game, as mine gets tanned and ruddy. I wouldn't believe that, and King said to me, "Simon and the Professor couldn't find a horse trail if you rubbed their noses in it. I believe that Buck has landed." So I sent him off with Jack on the same search. It was after ten o'clock, but in an hour, Miller appeared alone, tracking the boat up the bar, while Jack and King were driving the lost beast up through the brush on the north shore. Shot out by the current from the drift-pile, he had landed where the Professor said that landing was impossible, and had not looked. It takes a lot to kill a cayuse. All was a sort of roast for the Professor, and I think he felt it.

Now he is fussing about, a bunch of shaving paper tied to his breast pocket, stroking every one the right way, and talking with beautiful optimism about how very soon we'll reach the pass which we must cross in the main Alaskan Range, south of McKinley, before striking northeast along its northwest face, to the foot of the great mountain.

We still have fifty miles of wet country to cross, due north to Keechatna River, which we must ford to its north bank, following it up due west to the pass. The boat, thus, is going back down the Skwentna, till it meets the Yentna, a northern tributary; up the Yentna, to its western branch, the Keechatna, up that, to the head of navigation, where we meet and again ford the horses; put all the outfit on them, abandon the boat, and hit for the pass. Thus it travels three sides of a parallelogram, while the pack train covers its fourth.

The Professor, who must learn packing some day, is going to stick with the boat, still taking with him Miller, whom I want in Simon's stead with the horses. When I asked for Miller, he smiled, "You have got on so excellently as you are, I think we'll try it so again."

The gondoliers say that they had fair sledding on the river, though the 'skeets were cruel. The Professor confided that once he thought Miller would yield up his soul to their tortures, and propounded a weird theory that their poison in the big doses we get, injures and depresses the blood. As usual, where Siwashes and Tyonek men foretold good traveling, it was bad, and vice versa; and the awful canyon just above this camp—one of the country's bugbears, which they poled to this morning—was calm and navigable. So runs the glass of Alaskan truth and lies....

I am writing by a driftwood fire on the open sand and gravel of the bar. Boxes and tins on the silt-powdered logs tell of the ease of boat-travel. The Professor has set up an elaborate tripod, and is doing things with one eye to a white mountain of the Talkeetna Range upstream, which he is going to name. Think of that! I wish he would show quality of some sort. He's so kind and colorless. I like him—but then, I haven't hit the trail with him yet. He's just given me a pair of bedroom slippers "to wear about camp," he says. I thanked him. He uses "How?" instead of "What?" when you ask him a question.

JULY 9.—So here's the first day ended on the trail, where Brooks got cold feet last year, and said that King must hit for the hills, or the Government would have no more horses.

We had only four beasts down at once, two mired in beaver dams, two snagged in a sort of pitfall....

We've built six smudges, for here in camp the big, yellow-bellied horse-flies blacken the birches. I've been drying the tea that was on

Dark Buck when he floundered about in a mud-hole. It's shaving-time for the reflector. King, having climbed a tree to inspect the country ahead, is running straws through the big flies, saying as they sail aloft with wispy kite-tails, "That's how I like to serve you gentlemen." Jack is making a pipe from a birch-log, and Simon is giving us some rigmarole about Ricardo and Malthus, which no one is listening to.

We're in a plague—green inch-worms. Jack has just looked up in forgetful surprise, and said, "What's that dropping sound all around?" Drying blankets, you have to pick off hundreds to avoid roasting them—*en blanquette.* They form a scum on the packs. Every leaf and twig they have eaten; the alders and willows are pestilence-stricken. The whole country now seems wintry, now burned over, as they hit the high places for the birches. Their webs blind you on the trail, as you fish for them down your back. We have to eat in the tent. At supper, Simon counted thirteen on the inside of the canvas, and after a thorough house-cleaning. "That's unlucky for the worms," said he, squashing them with his spoon.

But I hear the sputter-sputter of boiling Bayos—covered, let's trust—so all's well on earth to-night.

JULY 10.—Jack carried out his threat and sneaked Simon's mosquito hat into the fire this morning, while the kid was brushing his teeth, or drying his socks, or doing one of the thousand useless stunts he devises while we're at work. He began crying for it as we cinched Brown B horse. Funny, but no one knew, as King said, "where it had went to." So Simon sprigged himself out with ferns till he looked like a hayseed, and as he puffed through the worst swamps, Jack hollered, "Say, Jerushy, haow's the crops?"

In one, where sweet bay grew with buckbrush from the sphagnum, suddenly McKinley, Foraker, and the whole range flashed out, seeming to float in mid-air over the haze, like magic icebergs. They lay between Yenlo Mountain—a low peak east of the Yentna, up which the Professor and Miller were to be plugging to-day to get a good look-see at the valley—and the nearer, opalescent peaks of the great range to the west, where we hope to enter it. Still square-shouldered and massive, each was tricked out wonderfully with cloud and shadow in rocky interstices unimaginably cold and deep, with ridges of bewildering lift and sweep, and a whiteness unknown to earthly snows. Southwest of Foraker, Mount Russell lifted a perfect concaved spire. Simon saw them half an hour after every one else, stopped the train, and ran up to announce his discovery. "I told yer," said Jack. "He's got eyes sharper 'n a tool-house rat, now he's no net on." And we must pass far to the west around them, getting our next view from their other side.

The next minute Jack exploded. The horses I drove balked. He was just ahead, and stooped for a drink. Quickly they tromped over him, though I yelled a halt. He cursed me furiously. Soon he was right behind when I had two beasts mired. I asked him not to drive his brutes over me. He shouted, "By ——, I'll give you some of your own medicine. Git up!" … At noon he was still peevish, and when I asked him to come over where Fred and I lay in the long slough grass, spitting tobacco-juice into a little stream, he shouted something about a "rotten, —— lunch," and didn't budge. And *we* were eating a can of mildewed prunes!

Which all reminds me of what Jack said yesterday, and I wanted to digest before recording. As we pulled away from the Skwentna, he came to me, almost humbly, and suggested that he go back to the Inlet in the boat with the two Indians, when we leave it on the Keechatna and put the whole outfit on the horses. "You only have grub enough for five men," said he, "and it won't last the six of us." "Darn the grub, there'll be enough," I said. "Isn't the real reason you want to quit because you're sore on the outfit?" "It makes me sore how Simon always spits on me," he answered. I couldn't get him to cite an instance of that, but I knew he meant the times when the kid jollies Jack about having been a plumber. Appearing disturbed and

disappointed, I urged Jack to stay on, putting my desire on the personal basis—the true one—on which he came with us, getting no
pay. He said that he was pleased with the way I had treated him. I
said that he couldn't expect us all to know how to shift up here as
well as a sour-dough like him. He said that he realized that—
though you'd seldom think so from his acts. He added that King was
sore on the outfit, too, and would have quit long ago, only he felt he
was "sort of contracted with the Professor." That from King doesn't
worry me. He likes to air our troubles, aggravated by the stress of
travel, to any one; and Jack he's naturally most in sympathy with.
But King will never quit us. I was telling Jack frankly that I was disappointed in him, when the Professor hove in sight, and I lit out as
Jack repeated the short-grub plaint to him. Simon, who had seen us,
wanted with excited suspicion to know what Jack had been saying.
"Oh, nothing," said I.

Spite of all, I do mightily enjoy Jack's company. There's something very compelling about him, and no malice nor yellowness
whatever. He's simple. Yet I think that of the crowd, except Simon
whom we can never lose of course, we could best spare Jack. I can't
let personal wishes block the expedition's success. I remember how
I laughed at Simon when once he said that Jack wouldn't see the
game through. Again, I read men wrong....

On we fought through worms and flies, having at most three
horses down. Now, all their tails are swishing furiously outside the
tent, and soon we'll hear them clattering through the dishes. Simon
must be homesick. He's been showing me the pictures of his pa and
ma, which he keeps with his eye-wash, tooth-wash, nose-wash, and
the rest of his drug outfit in that little bag. G———!...

The beast munching grass at my ear is fouling the guy-ropes.
King sleeps. Jack is reading the *Fortnightly Review*—and I can imagine the scornful comments he's making to himself at its long-
winded phrases.

The tag of verse to-day, was:

> One thing is truth, and all the rest is lies;
> The flower that once has blown forever dies.

I think it's from "The City of Dreadful Night." Wish that philosophy applied to yellow-bellied horse-flies, too. Good-night.

JULY 11.—To-day, Brooks' blazes (we see about two a day) kept leading us three miles forward, then three miles straight back. We couldn't lose countless slews of the Yentna, which infuriated Jack, so he sulked continually and wouldn't eat our stale biscuit and drink the stagnant glacier water in the long swamp grass stirred by the horses at the noon halt. Yet—"Say," he'd shout later, laughing as by chance we took to high ground, "we've gone wrong. There's more water over there." The Government topographer that King says blazed for Brooks must have reasoned in circles. Any drunk could have crossed this stretch drier and straighter. At last we skirted a quiet lake among strange little hills and sprucy meadows lined with otter trails, creeping close to its rock shore, thinking our troubles passed. . . .

Never! This can't last much longer. Zzzzzz-Zzzzzzzzz!—meaning the yellow-striped flies. It makes you dizzy to watch them swarming over the kicking brutes. Jack and King make caustic cracks about God's mean notions in creating them. They're as big as bumble-bees, still crusting sunny sides of the birches. Eight smudges surround us, and here in the tent, I squash them through the canvas, roosting in bunches on the outside. The slew-water—and a quarter mile away, too; we're a mile beyond the lake—stains the bean juice thick and purple as ink. The swish of horse tails is incessant. There go the brutes now, fouling the guy-ropes, giving the tent *d. ts.* The flies are driving them *wild*. King says they can't stand another day of this. Half the hair is eaten off their necks and haunches, and you can grab the pests off their faces in handfuls dripping with blood. The strain on any one with human feeling is dreadful. I never realized before how animals can suffer.... Bang! There they go again, clattering through the dishes. Stamp! stamp! stamp! Hobbled, they couldn't graze enough, and would burn their hoofs in the smudges....

A 'skeet in my ear is driving me wild. Jack has blown tobacco smoke into it, and Simon squirted in strong tea through a pipestem. We're praying for rain.

JULY 12.—Answered. Alone, as usual, I rustled breakfast in the drip, fighting slow 'skeet torture for an hour before another hand stirred.

Two miles!—and all around grinned the sick spruces and punctured sphagnum of tundra, and tundra in the rain, all humps and gridded with moose trails is the boudoir of Hades. In, out, and around we floundered; hunting leads, scattering the train, till Jack and I missed the lean Bay Dunnage mare, and then lost ourselves hunting her in the maze of tracks. Sense of locality—which maybe I'm losing anyway—all went to pot. Simon yawned, rested, and unpacked the White Grub horse to make himself coffee. King walked almost back to camp, having wrongly counted but thirteen tracks in the mud of the last slew crossed. I found the beast at last, and back-trailed for King, wearing out my neck shouting. He wasn't at camp or on the trail. So *he* was lost. Again, responsibility helped the 'skeets bite. That ghastly four hours! till Fred appeared calmly—I couldn't hear his tale—and we struggled on.

Suddenly King swore that we were but two miles from the Keechatna, his elastic memory now stretching the right way. And as our hearts rose, the beasts, of course, struggled into the worst swamps yet. The river had flooded meadows belly-deep. Across, we half-swam to an alder swamp that Satan must have sat up night a-plotting; there to re-act all the desperate old tragic stunts. Down went four beasts together in soupy mud-holes, snagged in roots, worming necks under big logs. Jack and I worked like beavers at the old tricks of kicking their eyes and watering nostrils, till they gurgled serpent hisses, and prodded heels waved. King chopped out the snags under their stomachs, deftly avoiding nicking off any chunk of flesh. We hauled on stiff and mud-hid cinches, fought with soggy grub and gritty-wet blankets, in repacking, at last. And not fifty yards away, swirled the brown tide of the Keechatna—our haven! "A man that 'ud take horses on a trail like this," yelled Jack, his temper switched to the antipodes at the reaction, "they'd lynch him in the Valdez country! I'd help to do it, too."

Now, we're lying on three solid feet of spruce boughs spread on soggy quicksand, yet sloshing our backs in the ooze if we move— the worst camp made yet. You could cut the air in this tent, thick with the stink of sore-rubbed horse-blankets which we must sleep in, and the mosquito-corpse fetor of never-washed clothing. Rheumatism numbs my side. Where's the Professor? He ought to meet us here now. Eaten by 'skeets and green worms on Yenlo Mountain, I guess. Well, here's for a page of "Tom Sawyer," to bring on drowsiness—but sleep, never!

JULY 13.—After two pages last night, I heard voices, and jumped up with Jack. Miller and the Professor were landing from the boat. It was bright eleven o'clock. "The —— of a time to be traveling," growled King. They had climbed Yenlo the day before, eating gophers—picket-pins, King calls them—while the 'skeets ate them. They'd failed to cut out the creatures' scent bags, such as muskrats have, and Miller was still coughing and spitting from their delicious taste. "Yes, we observed McKinley and Foraker from the top, and I obtained a very excellent idea of the country," said the Professor. He needed it. I said that I was glad.

They were satisfied with eating cold rice and tea. We shunted them from crowding into our tent, helped the Professor pitch his conical silk affair on the only dry inch of ground for miles, and I rustled him boughs in the dark. I saw him work for the first time.

Miller says that in the boat he sits and steers, never poling or track-ing, always having to try both sides of his paddle before he discov-ers how to veer the way he wants. Ashore, he still fusses with his instruments. Both, and even the two Siwashes, wore 'skeet hats. I was ashamed....

This morning we swam the horses to camp on the north side of the river, leading one by one behind the boat. Tiresome, but no more Skwentna games for us.

Simon is beginning to take notice about cooking and packing. He mixed all the panniers up to-day, angering me, and Miller dryly observed, "I've read about such fellows as him, but I never thought I'd see one." "I call him the fifth wheel," said Jack, "and have noted it to that effect in my diary." He tried to put fruit in the dried onion bag. Now the onions go in their own sack to-morrow, or Simon goes into the river. Fred got much joy out of the kid's wanting to pack last night's spruce boughs across the river for to-night's camp. He and Jack always build a big drying-fire after supper, and wall it in with blankets hung on cinches. When Simon, who can't light a fire to save his neck, hangs his wet pants on their lines, they're promptly thrown off. They dried three pairs of blankets for me to-night—an unheard-of compliment.

The Professor fusses, fusses, fusses with his instruments, which he carries in two big boxes, that will make trouble when we begin to pack everything. He opens a plush case, peeks in, wipes off the brass, closes case again—and there you are. That's hitting the trail real hard. That's scientific exploring.

All the food is soaking, yet no one but me seems to worry. All day I've been trying to dry it with fires, and cook Alaska rapid-fire, smokeless strawberries—meaning beans—at the same time. The sugar is syruping, and the bacon's mildewed. This is the first day in seventeen that we have rested, and King has lost his rubber shoes....

To-morrow, we strike west up the Keechatna, hoping to find, in about a hundred miles, a pass leading through the Alaskan range to its northwest face. Brooks found one, and Captain Herron in 1899, navigating to this point in a launch, found another. Across the mountains, he nearly died of starvation.... Our boat, with the same crew, taking everything but the bacon and the seven sacks of flour, will follow the horses till the river gets too swift. On both sides its meadows are flooded four feet deep; worse than last year, says King of tricky memory.

And still it rains. We'll be growing web feet and feathers yet.

JULY 14.—The worst day yet, King says; but I was too dazed, cold, and wet to feel it. The horses had starved all night. They crossed a slew to a grassless island in the still-rising river, and were too foolish to wade back, so I went swimming after them. We even put the bacon into the boat, and the seven flour sacks went singly on the seven strongest horses, the worn-out others carrying only their saddles. And the hippodrome swim through grass and willow meadows, to the first dry land, ten miles up-river, began.

I really lost my temper with Simon for the first time. Once, crossing silt and quicksand, where the water roared through willow roots to fill inland ponds, and one minute you had a footing and the next ducked in up to your neck, he shouted, and halted the train. I couldn't hear what he said, the river roared and the horses sloshed so. I called "Hello!" again and again. He didn't answer, but when at last I went to move on, there he was, only five yards off. He'd deliberately kept me up to my neck in the icy water. I swore at him. He moved on sullenly.

Then Jack lost the Light Gray. I went back alone, and found her right in the middle of the trail, up to her neck in mud, wedged between roots. Got her out, and fell plumb into the river myself. She mired herself three or four times more, and once I thought was a goner. Poor little beast! She loses her head in tight places, and struggles as if crazed. It's fearful when they close their eyes, lay their necks in the mud, grunt comfortably, and never try to shake the 'skeets crusted on their necks.

Later we swam the whole bunch, riding them, across a deep slew, and climbed a wooded terrace to camp. Half an hour after, the boat landed....

I've been urging the Professor to appoint duties and organize some system of camp and pack work. Jack and Fred are beginning to kick, and justly, with a do-nothing like Simon along. An expedition like this won't run itself. Unless its head, as I've been trying to do, sets an example by getting up first, starting breakfast, and leading tirelessly in every job, he's got to give orders, or growling begins. I told the Professor this. He will neither order, nor lead. He just fusses with his aneroids—junk, I call it all—and like most tenderfeet, is a continuous boot-changer. Simon butted in during our talk, so I observed that the 'skeets were pretty thick, and lit out. I've talked over this system business with King and Jack, which may not be right and loyal, but they and Miller agree with me. I've a mind to lie abed and just see what happens if I don't get up at five-thirty tomorrow and start breakfast. But I know that when the moment comes, I'll be on deck, and it will be up to Fred and me, in addition, to bake the two reflectorfuls of bread, cook, wash dishes,—Lord, everything! First must come success of the expedition, not my ideas, or even justice. The Professor ought now to be balancing side-packs against to-morrow, if he's really to run the pack train as he says he will, for everything is to go on the horses, and Jack is coming with us, having decided to without discussion or advice. Instead, our chief's down there by the river, praying over his junk, smiling at screws and nickel cases, lifting, stroking his old Abeny level. I no longer ask him to show quality; I wish he'd show something. He's too silent; hopeful without being cheerful; slow-witted.

I suppose I am a kicker, but is anyone ever quite responsible in this racket? Oh, well, now I've bitten off such a lot I might as well chew it without frothing at the mouth. My back aches from leaning over these pots. Wonder if I'm roasted in the others' diaries. I ought to be....

Queer how these slogans of travel vary. To-day I muttered over and over:

> Lizzie Borden took an axe,
> Hit her father forty whacks,
> When she saw what she had done,
> She hit her mother forty-one.

Fred sings:

> Over the slew
> The packtrain flew—
> Over the slew
> The packtrain flew.

CHAPTER VIII

Disaster and the Stoic
Professor

July 15.—We woke gasping for air, like trout on a bank, for the rain glazes a tent's pores, and makes it air-tight, but never mosquito-proof. At three o'clock, I moved under the Professor's silk, which was black with the vampires. They'd driven him into the open, mummied in blankets, but didn't faze me.

Miller helped at breakfast. Fred and I were ages adjusting packs, while the Professor vanished, writing to his wife, I guess. I scrawled a few lines home, and gave it to the Indian boys, who dropped down the river with a little grub and some of our superfluities, in the fold-ing kettle and night-lamp style, bound for the trading-post on Sushitna River. Simon delayed us by the school-girl trick of cutting birch bark to write home on.

We started at ten-thirty, cutting trail west, straight up the river-bank, with all the world holds for us gathered together at last, and overburdening the poor, tuckered, fourteen hairless brutes. Jack and King chopped trail ahead, the Professor leading the train with the big bay branded L.C. groaning under the junk boxes, which are a crime to pack on a horse. He has the easiest job—no brutes to drive, unmuck and recinch—but it looks important. Then come four horses, then Simon lazily moving his fat little legs, shouting when they're stuck, just in time to drive them off the trail; then four more beasts, then Miller, tall and silent in khaki; then five, and yours truly, the peevish rear-guard.

The going was better, through willow slews and spruce flats, but the 'skeet sparks swept our necks, the poison of the squashed and dead irritating the raw far worse in the wet. The Alaska 'skeet carries a whetstone, and flies sharpening his stinger....

To-night, the Professor is sitting behind the blanket-wall of Jack's fire, asking such questions as, "What trees are those across the river?" (Cottonwoods, of course.) And about distances and directions which any child with a map of Alaska could answer. He shows his gold front tooth as he smiles so slowly. Miller is reading Jack's "Pelham." Jack is laying down the law—and all wrong—about the difference between blueberries and huckleberries. Simon is putting a new ventilator into the tent, making Fred very sore by thus keeping him from going to bed. The wind's cool and from the North. Well, I must water the beans....

I scent trouble with the horses. They're playing out, and no denying it. We eased the loads of the Whiteface and Brown mare while crossing to the Skwentna, for one had got very thin, and the other lay down in the trail wherever she could. All are losing flesh fast, and the hair that the flies dug out isn't growing again, and more's falling. They stand around near camp, staring dazedly at us instead of rustling grass. Worst of all, their legs are swollen to double natural size.

"Just you see," said Jack in the Professor's hearing to-day, "another day in these snags and mud-holes, and good-bye to this pack train." King assented, but not before the Professor. In his hearing, Fred only shook his head, and said that the beasts did look mighty poorly. I know that what he *thought* was worse. He's the greatest diplomat I've ever known. It's impossible for him in all this stress to offend, even to disagree with any one to his face—except Simon, whom he joshes.

JULY 16.—It's happened—the expected! But prefaced by the Professor's funniest shine yet.

Fording a tributary to-day, Big Buck, behind whose pack he'd jumped, dumped him sprawling in midstream. Away floated his mosquito hat (which we haven't dared burn) and he after it, jounced along on the bottom bowlders. He's sure a peach. "When do we cross the Keechatna again?" he gurgled to King, crawling ashore. He thought that the creek was the main river, and he on a scientific expedition to map the wilderness. But I suppose it was a great loss, that mosquito hat, and he was dazed. So he tied a red bandanna handkerchief over his ears, and now looks like a Bashi-bazouk.

We climbed a ridge hinting of foot-hills hid in the rain, and nooned in a tundra. Again exotic park lands silenced us, luxuriant birches drooped, uncanny lush meadows waved deserted and unscarred, neck-deep with red-top. We drove on. Tundra suddenly. I was thinking how the swamp smell of Labrador tea oppressed me—suggesting, somehow, dead flesh—when ahead I heard Miller shout and shout to the Skinny Bay horse—the Moth-eaten Bay, we call him, he has lost so much hair. I saw Miller stop, but keep on beating the brute. No use. He wouldn't move. I ran up. I jabbed him with my stick. It only peeled off chunks of skin and hair. He had played out; now he spread his legs, trembled, lowered his head and blinked stupidly. I got Jack and King, and we unpacked him, carried his load, and led him to camp by the swamp-side.

Fred said, "He wouldn't have played out if I'd done with the horses as I wanted." I reminded him that on the fourth day out from Tyonek I had suggested laying over, and said that I never used to travel in the rain. To which he had replied, "It won't hurt them to travel every day, even a little, so long as you keep going"; which was characteristically meaningless. He says now that the horses have been worked too hard in a very bad country.

I repeated all this to the Professor, adding that a rest of two or three days here was imperative, as the Whiteface, Dark Buckskin, and Bridget, the white cook-horse (Miller named her) are on the verge of collapse. The Professor sighed, "Um!—de-um-de-ay!"

King says that if we keep on to-morrow, we'll never make the pass. I asked him what he'd do if this were his outfit. He answered: "Rest here a few days, and go on slowly, making short hour travels, adding a half-hour each day, if the horses pick up." I said, "Tell the Professor that. He expects you to. That's why you're along." He said, "I won't unless he asks me what I think. I'm only hired." I said that I'd tell the Professor all this, in that case. "Of course, it 'ud be different," added King, "if he'd put getting the horses through safe entirely in my hands." "I thought he had," said I, surprised. "He never said nothin' about it," answered Fred. "What I said about the horses with the Government last year, went. No one ever said, 'Isn't the' a better place a little further on?' when I said we had to stop to rest the horses, the way the Professor did last night."

The Professor says that we'll pull on to-morrow. I've promised the crowd that we shan't. The man hasn't the least idea of a horse's needs, nor of Alaskan travel. King is so afraid of giving offense, he won't express any more opinions at all. Yet he's anything but mild when it comes to grub, or dulling the axe....

JULY 17.—Sixth day of rain—and we haven't moved. I asked the Professor to come out and look at the horses with me, but he wouldn't. What do you think of that? His pack train is going to the devil, and he doesn't pay the least attention. Still just packs and unpacks his instruments. I wonder if he can use a theodolite, after all.

King and I went out to the beasts, he knocking the Professor and the outfit, saying that the horses were never fit for Alaska, anyway.

"I wouldn't have looked twice at that bay mare for this country, if I'd had the picking of this train," he said. "Yes, sir, we'll be lucky to get to the pass at all." But you can't always take men like Fred at their forecasts. Facts, which they're always swearing by, often turn out to be only what ought-to-be, or they fear-may-be.

The brutes' legs were still very swollen. That's the chief trouble, caused by snags on that first wet hike up-river. They seemed dazed, too. So are we. We're all depressed and grate on one another—and perhaps I do nag Simon too much.

The Professor has just observed that we may expect steady rain till we cross the pass. "Yes, and steady rain on the other side, too," snapped back Jack. He has never a word to say now about our troubles, quite dropping out as a factor in the outfit. Sometimes he and King have long whispered talks. Plots of mutiny! 'Sdeath! I had silly words with Jack at supper. Proud of his camp craft, he advises you how to do everything about it, as if he were commanding. I was adjusting the dough-full reflector in a hole before the camp-fire, when he said, "You'll have a —— of a time baking bread there." "Why, no," said I, "the reflector 'll tip forward and give the biscuits a better crust." He contradicted violently, so in my most exasperating way I faked a "scientific reason"—something about radiating angles of heat—to support me. He assailed me violently for "all your —— scientific views" (as if *I* ever had any). The reflector was burning my fingers, and I said, to get rid of him, "Haven't you any blankets to dry to-night?" "That's none of your —— —— business!" he yelled, before the whole hungry crowd of us.

Blanket-drying is a sore point with Jack. He and King steal away from camp work these rainy nights to their drying-fires, excluding Simon. Once, after dish-washing, I built a big one. "What yer doing that for? There's plenty of fire over here for you," called Jack. "It's no trouble to build a fire," I answered. (It was, though, in the wet, and I lied.) "Now, everybody come here to dry his blankets," I said. Jack growled something about my getting huffy when he'd invited me to his fire. I answered sweetly. A gentle answer does turn away wrath, except from Jack. He has hardly spoken to me since. Silly, aren't we? But he has worse tiffs all the time with Miller and Simon, which are none of my business. He and the Professor hardly ever speak....

Clearing mists are lifting threadily over the strange green hills northward. The Professor is lisping about eating seal and penguin and killing pelican in the Antarctic. Miller is crouching low out on the tundra, stalking what yells like a raven, but he calls a goose. "I'll eat it raw if it ain't a duck," said Fred. Simon is everywhere. We bore one another. I'm thinking, "Next trip, I'll avoid such a human combination as this." Suppose all the rest have said that to themselves, too....

Shall we move to-morrow? The Professor hasn't peeped about it. King still agrees that the only thing to do is to rest here a while to let the horses pick up, and then drive only two or three hours a day. Otherwise, the whole jig is up. I've told Miller, who has been ordered to build the fire these mornings—the first command yet given—not to be too hasty about getting up to-morrow. The Professor may find his mind in the night. I'm determined we shan't travel yet....

Oh! the silent reaches of wavy grass in this overnourished region; it's like the parks of carefully gardened English manors—but vacant, tragic. The immense drooping birches peel off great scrolls of bark; huge dead trunks waste away in the rainy luxuriance. For years they rot whitely before no human eyes. The dead spruce falls and is buried in moss, but the birch's ghost is imperishable....

JULY 18.—Seventh day of rain. We count as Noah must have. The Professor said nothing about moving, so here we are still. Again he wouldn't look at the horses. He doesn't seem to give a darn. Their legs are less swollen, and five galloped off when they saw me. They haven't done that for days, so they're better, except the Moth-eaten

Bay, who was caught in an alder thicket, and couldn't eat till I turned him out.

Pull out to-morrow? No one knows. The Professor says we'll "try it, and see how it goes." The devil of a principle! We've got to run this team on some system, or we're done for. The Professor won't tell if we're going to travel two hours or twenty. He can't make up his mind. Can't seem to grasp the situation. I protested that we shouldn't hike for more than three hours, anyway. "If we do that, we might as well stay here," said he. Logic, eh?

Simon is ordered to help Miller cook breakfast every day, Jack and King to get supper. Jack growls at having to eat Simon's cooking; says that the kid doesn't wash himself enough. We should be more cheerful, but we're not. We have no common sense of humor. Jack and the Professor have none at all; King's is rooted in queer little repartees and rhymes, and Simon's in bad puns. I've been told mine is pretty badly distorted, too. But I'd like to hear a good, hearty laugh, even my own.... Miller is playing checkers with Simon on a pencil-marked board on the kerosene can. Jack is reading a Government Survey report. The Professor, having just broached a scheme to cut off distance by finding a pass north of Brooks', is fussing, fussing, fussing—!

JULY 19.—So we started. Bridget, the cook-horse, was down on his knees before we'd gone three hundred yards, not mired in the swamp, but played out. I shouted, and ran forward, suggesting we return. The Professor, who was 'way ahead of his train, wouldn't hear of it. He and Simon tried to bat the brute up. I wouldn't hit him, nor would Jack or Fred. When a horse knees down, he's failed, and no amount of banging his skull with a club does any good. I hate the cayuse for a mean, sly, contrary beast, but I won't stand by and see any warm-blooded animal tortured when it's at the end of its rope.

I could hear Simon's monotonous "git up"—he's mighty handy at beating horses to show off to the Professor—and Miller curse him for hitting the poor brute on his head with the butt of a pole. At last they seemed to have got him up.

Twenty yards on, a flooded creek flowed through willows. Bridget and three others went down. This time, Miller refused to help; and Jack and I held off till we saw the beasts would suffer worse in the mud. "No one seems inclined to aid," said the Professor. We pulled them out without beating, and King filled the worst mudholes with brush, complaining the while to me of Simon's and the Professor's brutality. Somehow we got across, but had more mirings. In three hours the order was given to camp. So what I suggested does go. I think the Professor really intended to go only three hours, but pig-headedly wouldn't say so, not to appear to be taking orders from me. I hope he's beginning to realize the nature of a pack horse, and what we're up against in Alaska. I'd like to call this camp the Camp of the Dawn of Reason.

We're brighter. Yet hardly a third of the distance to McKinley has been covered, and we must reach the mountain by August 15th. After that, it will be too cold to climb, and grub will run out. Sack after sack of flour disappears, one each week, and one should last ten days. And the pass found by Herron and lost by Brooks is still ahead....

We've been arguing about the fable of the ant and the grasshopper. I took the cicada's side, and put it all over the ant as a mean, crusty beast, who had lost all capacity for enjoyment through blind, hard work, and therefore boiled at pleasure got by others. Somehow Jack was peevish, because Simon and I said we thought it a joke to call the white gelding "Bridget," and "she." Now he is reading "Tom Sawyer," and the Professor the *Fortnightly Review*—for the first time in his life, I guess.

So at last it has cleared in the windless, nerveless, Alaskan way. Clouds form here without motion in the glittery white sky; it rains a month; suddenly, still without wind or mist movement—it magically clears.

CHAPTER IX

I BREAK LOOSE TWICE

JULY 20.—My first brush with the Professor. I was tactless and hasty. Sorry.

We started, with no inkling of how long the skinny beasts must plug on. Through ghastly birches, grass which met over the tops of the packs, willow swamps, at last we met a box canyon of the foothills in three hours. It was pitiful, driving the beasts sheer down through the brush. Poor Miller gave up beating Bridget, I pelting mud from above. Somehow we did get him across the creek at the bottom. Then he spread his legs—played out again.

I was angry, ran ahead, and seeing the Professor, burst out about his having "sense knocked into him some time," knowing "nothing about horses, and not wanting to know." The torrent came too easily. "Dunn, it doesn't do any good to talk like that," he said quietly.

I went back with Simon, and we did bat Bridget along. Simon likes beating horses—when the Professor's around—but he left Miller and me to haul the beast up the opposite scarp of the canyon, on which Bridget rolled into a mud-hole. Miller and I unpacked him, back-packed his load to the top, and dragged him up to the Professor. "I'm sorry if I put my feelings too strongly some-times," I said to him. He only answered, "Dunn, you talk too much and too loud all the time." Now, on the way back to Bridget, I had cursed the Professor's leadership to Simon, who probably told him, or he had overheard—hence the "loud." Next, the Light Buckskin rolled off his pack, and we camped. Just three hours' travel again.

Yet, I'm happy to-night—if that can interest any one but the carelessly absent gnats. A strong wind blows. Over our swamp, sharp snow peaks, blue with the vague, questioning azure of the North, fuse whited spires into a burnished heaven. Evening casts queer shadows from the alder-clumps, into the rank grass and snow patches of our hill-sides....

Simon has actually volunteered to wash the dishes. Jack's punching holes in a tin plate to sift the lumpy, mildewed flour; some of its yellow and green chunks are big as half-a-dollar. I'm drying grub.

At last! I've just asked the Professor to take us more into his confidence, and he announces beforehand—think of that!—that we'll only travel three hours a day till the horses are better. Victory!

JULY 21.—We hit down good trailing through alder to the dozen silty channels of the Keechatna. All the beasts are better. The Brown mare didn't lie down once. I drive the train's rear still, with the six worst invalids to bat on; Roan, Whiteface, Bridget, Moth-eaten Bay, Big Buck. Fred says they've had "distemper," which means any old disease; the Professor that they were poisoned by the yellow-bellied flies, since they played out so suddenly. I remember that at Tyonek Light Buck and Little Gray had foul breath and ran at their noses; so others did at the Skwentna. The Moth-eaten and Dark Buck still have hardly a hair on their bodies, and couldn't live a minute among flies. Now the sickest are the Brown B horse and P.R. Sorrel, who carries and is always shipping that box of Simon's with his botany presses in—which Jack and I are planning to "lose"—so you can't blame the P.R. Light Buck and Little Gray haven't shown a sign of failing, so may not they all have only been suffering in getting acclimated, these two recovering from their dose first?

King, though he's willing to say "Yes" to any one's suggestion, except Simon's, to whom on principle he pays not the least attention, agrees that the train is saved. . . .

Nine o'clock, and the sun is poised magically over translucent mountains in the west. Miller is using them in queer calculations with guess-work angles and his watch. The Professor is loafing, of course. He wears the cut-off tops of his socks for wristers to keep the 'skeets out, and instead of the Bashi-bazouk handkerchief, a golf cap, so he looks like a yellow-haired Bluebeard.

JULY 22.—In four hours we have made ten miles, hitting the tangled river channels, which we "took across," as King says, fording incessantly from bar to bar. Simon, who seems to care for nothing but his own comfort, hates to wet his feet. At one fording, he jumped behind one of his bunch's pack, dashed among the rest, scattering them till they were swimming about and wetting the grub. The horses made back to shore, and from the other side he refused to recross and corral them, which Miller and I had to do. At the next channel, he cut into the middle of my bunch on a narrow spit, and drove the P.R. back a quarter mile. He fetched her, and caught us at the next ford. All his beasts had plunged in ahead, so he sprang to ride one of mine, but I batted them all on furiously, and though I slumped in to my armpits, Simon had to wade. We others, except the Professor, who has only L.C. to manage, always wade. It's the only way to safeguard dry crossings for the grub. Every one is sore on Simon for these tricks, especially Fred and Jack, for besides wetting the grub, he soaks their favorite blankets. He hasn't yet any control over a horse, nor seems to want it. . . .

Once to-day I had to laugh. The Professor carefully tied his money belt around his neck, dabbed at a channel, like a bear after salmon, with the old Siwash canoe paddle he found and carries—to find the water two feet deep!

Simon is more and more of a mark. No attention is paid to his comments. Fred reverses his every suggestion. This morning we wrapped the axe up in his hat, and he was nearly sunstruck. When he found the cap to-night, in camp, he simply said that we had played a "low trick" on him, and began to whine about having a headache. I hate meek people.

At last the box of hard-tack "for use on the mountain"—thus the cayuse revenges himself for mean packing—is bunged and wet, and we are eating the crackers, with some of the Professor's peanut brittle. I have stewed a mess of the green currants which grow everywhere, and like green apples, make better sauce than when ripe. Jack has just made a bull, getting very sore when every one laughed. "There's lots of trout in these muddy rivers," said he, "when they're clear." King and the Professor are filling empty flour sacks with dry grass, because those hefty junk boxes are chafing L.C. The beasts seem hairier and almost well; anyhow, they've just gayly tromped over my drying blankets. Simon is mending his pants, as he does every minute of every evening. Miller has just been imitating his shuffling walk, which is like the man's where I pawned my gold sleeve links in Seattle. He has spread his botanical paper in the sun. Can't we roll on it somehow?

JULY 23.—Simon keeps up his fording stunts. Though the days are all too alike, the dazing tension of travel never relaxes; herding horses one by one over miles of muck; boiling beans, mixing bread, burning callous fingers on the hot, collapsing reflector: never an hour to rest, to dry off from the tortures of rheumatism, mend tattered boots and clothes, forget the roar of icy water about your waist, the crazing cloud of 'skeets.

Ahead, indecently whiskered, the slightly knock-kneed Professor, in gray cap, gold-tooth, and goloshes, red handkerchief and paddle—

"The white, crackly desert... where we trudged for hours, seeming not to move." (Ascending Peters Glacier, Mt. McKinley.)

like the wand of a sour-dough fairy—yanks at unwilling L.C. Next, squirrel-faced Simon potters on, also with red handkerchief, and a little black velvet cap, that with his new, fuzzy black whiskers, makes him a sure-enough Yiddisher. Feebly he yells, "Git up! Git on there!" letting his four beasts lag 'way behind, jump from the trail into each mud-hole, scatter on the wooded bars, delay us. Still slim Miller, in broad-brimmed hat and brown canvas, yells at his beasts like an ox-driver, but lets me, the growler—not saying much, for responsibility's all up to the Professor now—know with my invalid pets when the trail's blocked, which Simon never does. Ahead of all, Jack and Fred still chop, curse, and rubber-neck through the willows, slump into the slews. So it is, up and down terrace, through swamp, across stony channel.

The valley is bending northward, narrowing 'twixt the green foot-hills paneled with snow. We're camped by the beaver swamp of a clear tributary. Miller and I started to fish. I got one yellow-belly fly for bait off Bridget, one off Whiteface, and a big grayling ate them at the first cast of the willow pole. Bacon drew only shy nibbles. The creek got too bushy, so I got busy with the geological hammer and a slate out-crop—the first rock we've seen since the Skwentna. I climbed the scarp, plunged into the creek's canyon, where a waterfall I saw would keep a summer hotel crowded at home; but nary a fossil. Miller had played Jonah, too, but was back at camp, stewing green currants. I've made that mess an institution. It saves our dried fruit, and the Professor says it's better for insides. Besides, it uses up lots of sugar, which I don't care for, and I shall take a sadistic delight in seeing our sugar hogs—we won't mention any names—suffer from its lack some day. . . .

Yonder is a grassy hill arranged with drooping birches. I bet you that a latticed summer house is hid somewhere on top; and that beyond, nestling in a valley, where men are making hay, dozes an ancient hamlet with white-steepled church. Do you wonder vacant Alaska drives some men mad?

JULY 24.—Jack is sick with a pain in his chest. The Professor says that it's neuralgia, and gives him white tablets. King says that Jack nearly caved in yesterday, and threatened to "lay down" on the trail, letting us go on without knowing. Though ill several days, he has confided in no one but King up to to-day, when, after crossing a large clear stream coming in from the north, he was weak enough to fall twice and be carried down with the current.

To-day the Professor had his first practical idea: that we'd make better time always traveling the mile-wide river-bed, endlessly fording the twisty channels which get narrower and swifter; which we've done. And though King wanted to keep to the hills, because Brooks had hugged them, and swore that the glacial wash skinned hoofs, we've come near sixteen miles to camp by this slew.

This morning we opened the lone can of glucose syrup, long yearned for by Simon. "G——, it's ambrosia!" gasped he at breakfast, wallowing with it on his pancake. Carefully he hid the can in the empty coffee-bag on Bridget's right-side alforgus. Now, I hate sweet-tooth gluttony on the trail, so when we unpacked Bridget to-night—no syrup can. Yes, that right pack had slipped coming down the scarp to camp; Miller and I had noticed it; even the coffee-bag hanging out! Nobly Simon quelled his tears, and all but started can-hunting on the back-trail. We got him to spoil his ambrosial appetite by eating a whole flap-jack under plebeian sugar, before fondly we produced the syrup from the grass where Fred had slung it. Isn't it a shame to horse the boy so? This is Alaskan humor, in a crowd like this.

The Professor rears his conical tent on the gravel bar, to dodge the 'skeets, he says, though I notice he's built a baby smudge, which he reaches in a rubber-shoe ferry. Miller's picking currants; I've shaved, and am mending my pants and drawers with dunnage-bag canvas, where the whole shebang had worn through to the skin kneeling before cook-pots. I have to do nearly as much cooking as ever. Simon never gets up in time to help mornings, but crawls out of his blankets just before Miller hollers, "Brek-faast!" and without washing, sneaks the first pancake off the pile. Just now, King and I are enlarging on how thick the 'skeets are in the tent—we've not been pestered with one for two nights—just to keep the kid from sleeping there. So, as he did last night, he's rigging a wicker hood over his bed with willows—near the grub as usual, I observe.

Jack sleeps. I wonder what would be done if any one were really laid up? The Professor hasn't a shadow of a notion, I'm sure. All day I had a bad pain over my appendix, so he said. It doesn't worry me. How could it? I can't imagine a man stranded on a rock in mid-ocean without grub or water *worrying* can you?

JULY 25.—Simon caught it to-day, and I'm ashamed again. Stubborn and vital he is, though maddeningly lazy, and slow as old women; yet compared to what might have been, and generally is, with such as we in Alaska, our hopeless and unending life is Arcadian. . . .

He kept up his tactics, leaping behind a packed horse at each ford, dashing across and scattering the train to swim in circles out of depth, soaking the precious grub. We swam a-thousand-and-one channels, pounded a-thousand-and-one gravel bars. Miller and I, getting angrier and angrier, stoned him through swift water, so he thumbed his nose at us. What do you think of a man who'll let an expedition go to keep his feet dry and then glory in it?

At last I got him. The icy water, hurtling bowlders along bottom, roared under our armpits; we made a blind island, and drove the beasts right back again. Simon mounted the Roan, as I chased, beating the horse with a stick. The kid lost his temper, and lunged at me in midstream, saying he'd "do" me if I hit his horse again. I did, of course. When we landed, he made a dive for me. We clinched, and in ten seconds he was lying on his face, chewing silt and gravel, making suppressed, back-handed lunges. His spectacles and hat were lost. I didn't want to hurt him, so he began taking it out of me in talk. The worst he called me was a cad and a bully. He was foaming at the mouth and weepy, making foxy struggles to get up if I relaxed, till I landed him in six inches of slough water, and said he could freeze there or promise not to ride channels. Miller added insult by coming along laughing and taking a photograph of us—as Simon promised. "You act as if you ran this whole outfit," he whimpered. "Whatever you do is right, but if any one else makes a break, you come down hard on them." I grieve that can't be denied.

Ahead, the Professor had stopped the train, and asked Miller what the trouble was. "Oh, only Dunn and Simon," he answered, "settling a small difficulty." The Professor said nothing, and won't. Soon, every one was being carried off his feet in the next channel, soaked and pounded on the white granite bowlders. Miller went down with a look on his face as if he saw the Angel Gabriel, and the Professor flopped about with his paddle like a giant Dungeness crab. Twice I slipped into holes over my head, and though never carried away, lost my hat, as my horse bunch hit back for shore. And Simon, deprived of pack horses, was all but shipped to Cook Inlet! I pulled him out with a pole. Talk about coals of fire!

Here in camp, we've been holding a post-mortem of the day. Fred baited Simon unmercifully, and Jack observed that he'd seen the fifth wheel washing gravel out of his hair. Simon was burning in a fry-pan his indigestible biscuits insides—the old trick—when King drawled, "What yer carryin' around that smudge with yer for?" Even the Professor added his mite by issuing the fiat that no more pancakes, on which Simon lives, are to be cooked, because they use too much sugar. Those two seem tuckered out, and now are asleep in the sun with their mouths open; not beautiful sights, with Alaskan crops of whiskers. I've said good-bye to my toes. For days they've been sticking through my boots, so I've capped them with leather from one of the two Abercrombie saddles, and Belgian nails. Our legs are badly chafed. We smear them with vaseline. Jack

is riveting a flour sack to his overalls. Miller can't find any currants....

Now we are discussing how Herron and Brooks crossed the
mountains. Brooks missed Herron's way—Simpson Pass—and found
another, more circuitous, leading him first back to Skwentna head-
waters. King remembers little about it all. We're hardly a day's travel
now from whatever glaciers the Keechatna heads in. "We must get to
work on a reconnoissance of Simpson's Pass to-morrow," says the
Professor, pompously. Everything we guess and prophesy about it
would drive you mad. Only higher and sharper tower these sudden
mountains, the To-toy-lon sub-range. Spruces cling only down along
the river, which is a single, mad, chocolate thread. To-day we passed
the first bunches of glaciers hid in jagged, slaty peaks, direfully
folded and faulted, pitching with snowfields and greenery strewn on
their desert tali, sheer from the roar below here. Old nature, grand
style, is getting busy.

CHAPTER X

PLEURISY AND THE PASS

JULY 26.—Rain! We're shivering in the ever-wet blankets, at the last rotting cottonwoods—tree line. You could cut the tobaccoey air in the tent, made by King's and my pipe-tobacco-and-botany-paper cigarettes. Thus we pipe on, and rag-chew, about what Brooks did, Herron did, and we'll do.

The country doesn't at all gee with Herron's map, and Brooks has discreetly left a blank where he got lost. From here, three valleys open into the peaks and snowy haze veiling Simpson Pass. The northernmost ends with the main source of the Keechatna, Herron's "Caldwell Glacier," for through the scud we can see a clear green river, like a pillar of malachite, streaking its smooth and ashen desolation. The central valley is narrow and unglaciated; the southern, which Brooks followed and went wrong in, getting lost for five days, is broad and has a *siltless* stream. If it leads to Simpson Pass, Herron's "Fleischmann Glacier" (he must have come from Ohio, scattering all these Buckeye politicians' names about) whose moraine he crossed, should lie in it; but glaciers should have silty streams. Fred tells how Brooks' topographer lost his temper with Herron's map, tore it up, and turned south out of this southern valley. It does seem the most logical to explore; yet the central valley, since we have found axe marks leading into it, ought to be tested, too.

Jack has just been very funny. Some one took his blankets left drying by the fire, and he let out ten yards of curses, shouting that if he found the man he'd "lick him, if I have to take a club to him." Came Miller's voice from the silk cone, "I got three blankets from under the tree." Looks to me as if the Professor'd swiped them and forced Miller into the breach. He was in the tent, too. No one fought.

Later.—The Professor and I have climbed the ridge between the two iceless valleys. He wouldn't go far, sauntering to pick blueberries, uming and ahing, clearing his throat, (Jack says that he must have some "fashionable" disease in it) losing the trail, choosing the worst places through the alders, and showing no sense of locality. He wasn't so hot to find that short cut north of Herron's Pass he was talking of when the beasts played out. He seemed even content to follow Brooks.

Once, squatting in the desolate dripping furze, high in the unearthly storm, he said: "I've spoken to Jack once or twice about these outbursts of his. Have you seen how queer his eyes are lately? They're like a man's who is going insane." I have noticed the hollow pallor of his cheeks, but they never hinted madness to me. Jack hasn't been able to lift a flour sack for days. No one dares now even comment on his words or actions, for he explodes at the simplest remark. "The fact is," ended the Professor, "I've decided that Jack has pleurisy, anyway, and not neuralgia." ...

The hollow river thunders. Fitful light thrills the valley into vast mosaics of green and gold. Never have I seen such jagged mountains, sheer slopes so blasted with broken black rock.

JULY 27.—Jack lay moaning by me all night, his hands pressed tight to his chest.

I took Miller and a baking-powder tin of burned beans, unsalted (the horses ripped open the salt sack this morning, and almost cleaned it up) to search the middle gorge. Just as we separated from the pack train, which went south through the broad valley, I saw Jack staggering up behind, his fists on his chest, gasping with pain. I ran ahead, and shouted to the Professor to stop and see Jack. "Yes, we'll let him have a tent alone, to-night," was all he said, never budging from L.C.

Miller and I struck off west. Far below in these hateful peaks where we struggled, up, up, along sliding talus, across snow-bridges, roared a feathery stream in a Titanic crack. Clouds rolled up from the coast, lit by strange flashes of sunlight, now dissolving, now creating more dizzy rock slopes, fingered with the startling green of alders, or blighted by mournful ice pushing down atrophied flanks from the endless storm.... Four miles, and we crossed a bigger snow-bridge. We divided the beans and our three biscuits, and shivered on water-swept talus among waxy alpine flowers at the range's heart. The gorge was blind; at least you'd have had to "lift yourself with toes and fingers" to reach the Kuskokwim valley, now our goal—as Herron writes that his Indians told him before deserting. We retraced our steps, and took up the whole day's journey of the pack-train. At last we sighted Big Buck nosing at the moss in a bend of the big south valley; then the Professor's cone house, and Simon alone, nursing a wet willow fire. Again the Moth-eaten Bay had played out!

Hungry as we were, Simon, when he saw us coming, though he had eaten only an hour back, seized the frying-pan and covered the only hot place in the tiny blaze to make himself pancakes. Gosh! Alcohol, sacred for use on the mountain, had to be used to light it, after even Jack, said the kid, had given up hope for a fire.

Jack was asleep, King and the Professor off looking for Herron's Fleischmann Glacier. Simon, for no particular reason, began firing his Colt smokeless to bring them back. Jack woke and cursed us all till the scouts returned, glum and shaking their heads. Yes, they'd seen Fleischmann, but no Pass: the valley ended blind. Should we stay here to reconnoitre to-morrow, or head southeast through Brooks' side valley, which we supposed was the one opening opposite camp—King didn't remember—at right angles to our gorge? I didn't believe that Herron went through here drunk, as you might have thought to hear some of us talk. I left camp, saying nothing. In half a mile, Fleischmann Glacier pushed its flat blueness out upon huge slate moraines. I waded its stream, siltless by some miracle, and mounted the bowlder-strewn esker. It appeared to wall a niche in the blind range. I rose, still keeping southwest; the walls seemed to slip apart; my heart was burning; a steeper, darker, valley opened—and, quite against all physiographic law, turned narrowly downward, bent further west among sharper, darker mountains truncated by cloud. The Pass! The Kuskokwim valley, illimitable, untrodden, unto the tundras of Behring Sea.

I ran down to slosh through its head-waters. Yellow and white Arctic poppies bloomed on the mossy shale. It was twilight. Where were the grizzlies that Herron wrote had chased him here? I had no gun. I was ready for them. How chary is life of such triumphs as this; what wonder men go to the devil, seeking in civilization to counterfeit such intoxication! But what had this not cost? In the easy order of the world, helpless man was meant for evil....

We're shivering in the tent. Jack is in with us, groaning. Some one said in Valdez, I remember, that he looked like the only one of us who could stand the racket on such a trip as this. Oh, very well. Talk of godforsaken camps! The cheese-cloth, dog-house door is open; only two 'skeets are clinging to the roof, too numb and discouraged, it's remarked, to do business. Across this old glacial valley, the haunting talus still sweeps into cloud. Two fuzzy bunches of alders, insanely green, lie between the dug-like black fans at their base, by the stream's sudden canyon. Below, there's a meadow—surely blue with wild forget-me-nots—where gulls from the sea are hovering.

Over there a man would seem a fly, yet you'd think that from here you could hear him whistle, but for the wind that's howling—so does the Alaskan scale of things upset all time and space. Furiously that wind bellies the tent. Like the Biblican house, I hope we've got rocks under.

We're to have one and a half biscuits apiece, already cooked, for breakfast, as a fire with the soaked green willows is impossible any more. Simon, who cooked them in the frying-pan, has burned all. You see, he likes them burnt.

JULY 28.—Alcohol lit the willows for breakfast tea, after Miller had tried two hours without it. When sure he wasn't joshing that they burned, we shivered out of the tent; ate, horse-hunted, packed, and headed for the Pass.

Jack started, walking ahead alone, groaning as he leaned on a pole. The Professor cavorted about, photographing us on a snow-bridge over the glacier stream. Down, down the talus of the Pass we slabbed. The horses balked at mashing hoofs to a jelly, so we herded them on the stampede, clattering all over the two thousand feet slope of chipped rock. Simon with his .22 popped a dozen times at a ptarmigan ten feet away, so Miller jumped in and wrung the bird's neck. At last the valley bent, and spruce trees—forgotten things—climbed from the coveted valley of Tateno River. Everyone was weary.

Six o'clock, and no camp; impenetrable willows, cross-canyons, packs slipping; and repacking is impossible, boiling river places was a rest. Seven o'clock—lucky the Moth-eaten Bay had no pack at all. Bridget slipped the reflector off his pack, and went bucking up a mountain with Light Buck. Even Fred, as we repacked, talked of the Professor's getting sense knocked into him some time about horses; and across the canyon, small as an ant, I could see how furious was Jack by his jerky motions. And Miller was sullen.

The immense bed and tiny stream of the Tateno met us at dusk; and camp is among strange red-berried bushes and moss powdered whitely with silt, far from the currants, rank grass banks and lush flowers of the rainier coast country. A new flora, new climate—now for new life!

"Why stop?" said I in my nastiest way, but thinking of the poor brutes. "I thought you were going to make the Kuskokwim to-night, Professor." And Jack, apparently mistaking such a josh for a real idea of the Professor's, went off at half-cock, as usual.

At last we've crossed the great Alaskan Range. When we have unwound from its heart, the last stretch to McKinley will be ahead. We follow down this tributary; then down the south fork of the Kuskokwim till it emerges from the mountains; then we turn northeast along their face, through the foot-hill country.

JULY 29.—The first day we rest, and are not forced to.

At breakfast we made out four sheep crawling like legged snowballs over the mountain back of camp. Off starts Fred with the Professor's .44. At noon, while ripping off the outer sacks from the flour, and laying all the grub in the sun—though it rains now and then—we hear shots, and count thirteen snowballs on the mountain skedaddling over a ridge, some down into a canyon, some up, some straight along; at last appears Fred wearily and doll-like up there, lucklessly following after. Down another gorge he sneaks; up merrily dash the four sheep on its far side. Shots sound; not a moving speck yonder. Appears Fred at last in camp, cursing the Professor's gun as "worn out" and "leaded." We try target practice, and it won't hit within two feet of the stump. So we called beans mutton, and ate glumly, as a snow-squall sugared the red peaks all about, and the aneroid marked us 2,590 feet up, the thermometer 51°. Summer's scarce this year.

Jack seems better, but only Fred dares ask after his health. He moves about glumly, eating little. "I'm afraid we must leave him behind—with grub, of course—till we return," the Professor has just said to me. "It appears a cruel thing to do, but what else is there?

Jack appears to be played out. He hasn't any more heart." It does seem so. But shall *we* return this way?

JULY 30.—Again we ford river channels, traveling south down the Tateno River to within three miles (we guess) of the Kuskokwim; shallow channels, so we let Simon, who is now trained properly, shin behind the Light Gray and save his feet. King seizes Big Buck, Miller the Brown B horse, Jack the Roan, I Whiteface. Each in turn we undo our beast's tie-rope, stone our charges through the treacherous current, follow wavering with the bowlders dragged along bottom. The Professor is the most comical spectacle ever, shinning with much leg motion behind his junk on L.C., leaning forward as if sick, his knees stuck in, his rubber feet out. He rides if the water's over his boot-soles. He can't decide where to ford, but leads L.C. in circles about each bar, till I shout nastily from behind, "Well! Well! Which way? Which way?"

Here in camp in rain, moss, and forest, for tundra has spread everywhere, and there's almost no grass, he has again begun harping to me about Jack. "I think Jack had better go back," he said. "He won't get any better wading all these rivers, and even if he does, he won't be of any use to us on the mountain. If he rests here a day or two, he'll feel apparently all well—well enough to cross the Pass and raft down the Keechatna. The pains in his chest will stop. He hasn't anything very dangerous; it's not septic pleurisy—" he went on in his conciliatory, querulous voice, accenting the last word in each phrase. The Professor is a sort of mild and gentle Teutonic Cedric or Ethelbert, long-haired and fair. After all, I can't be out of sympathy with him. But I suspected he simply wanted to get rid of Jack, as his usefulness as a horse-rustler is about over, and we haven't any too much grub. He even announced that Jack was going back. The crowd heard it in silence.

I wish I knew more about pleurisy. The risk of sending any sick man across that dismal Pass alone, to swim and reswim that mad

Keechatna, and raft two hundred miles, seems revolting and inhuman.

But here in the tent, Jack has brightened up at the prospect, and seems almost his old self again. He's pointing out childishly, and laughing in a queer way at one splash of mud on the wall that looks like a pig, one like an Uncle Sam. I've rustled spruce boughs for his bed, and told him that whatever he does must be of his own accord. He began magnifying the difficulties of a return in his childish way. "How does the Professor figure I'll take a back pack up that Pass with these pains? That's all I don't like—that Pass. He oughter told me I had the pleurisy before we crossed it. Won't I get worse wading those streams? And how can he spare enough rope for a raft? Suppose I lose one? The only man I knew had these pains spit blood and died on Copper River in '98," etc. He suggested he take the Moth-eaten Bay, who can only pack forty pounds, but would carry his blankets and clothes, take him across streams till water is deep enough to raft in, and his saddle would supply rope for the logs.

Later.—I put that very strongly to the Professor. He won't see it, cruelly, I thought, and said we'd need the Moth-eaten Bay to trade off packs in resting the other horses. But he can't ever carry enough for that, and as the grub goes, we need fewer horses, and this one is almost sure to starve going down the Kuskokwim, where King says there's no grass at all. "Well, I'll see what King thinks," the Professor evaded at last. I've tipped off Fred to kick at Jack's going back without the horse. I shall.

JULY 31.—First, the impossible happened. The Professor yawned out of bed before breakfast, and laid aside for Jack's return the small skillet, a can of milk, and a tin cup.

Then Fred and I began a five-mile horse-hunt. Somewhere on the weary tundra we met Miller, who said, "Jack is better, and coming with us to-day." "Seems to me," drawled Fred, "Jack takes on a little more about being sick than he ought. You never can tell from a man's looks how he'll stay it out up in this country."

In hours, we found Bridget and the Light Gray hiding on a remote summit; we packed; floundered out upon the measureless silt flats of the Kuskokwim, south fork, flowing due west; and followed its current. It was too deep to ford anywhere, so we labored seven miles down the north bank, wading slews in its flooded desert bed.

Camp is on a mossy spruce-flat. Rabbits are so thick they almost trip you up. Miller has shot a mess with his revolver.

The horses are vainly nosing about for swamp grass in dry tundra-puddles between us and a theatric mountain. So light is the snowfall, the ground here is always frozen, and dry sphagnum replaces lush grass. Crossing to here from the Keechatna is like going suddenly from England to Arizona. Southward, great canyons cut away toward the mist-ringed ice of regions utterly unknown; up-river drowse black, glacier-mantled peaks. Overhead spring the Terra Cotta Mountains (discreetly named so by Herron), clear-cut and youthful. The gray river-channels roar like falling rain in the dry sunlight, through dazzling silt and saffron willow flat. Yonder, a slow-eating fire blights the forest with insane designs. Its smoky spires meet undulating clouds above, suspended there like sea-grass in bright water....

Jack seems better adjusted to this queer crowd; and better physically, but still discouraged. For some time he's dropped his old sourdough scorn of our green ways. It's a good beginning, and must keep up if he travels on. But a trip for its own sake is never enough for him, who has never worked for anything but daily wages. I wonder why not? Possibly some subjective reason that I can't be bothered with these days. He seems to have deceived himself about the rewards of this exploration; and self-deceivers tire me; must not be taken too much to heart. Irishmen, anyway, can stir up amazing sympathy about nothing, and in the end fizzle out.

Simon, even as he complains of indigestion, eats his third cup of apricots, resugaring them which are already sugared in cooking. The Professor is a-sweetening up, too. Sometimes I think that they're peas from the same pod.

AUGUST 1.—After the magnificent horse-hunt—the Dunnage Bay found last under the very bench where the Professor was junking—Jack began confabbing, discussing, as most persons consider in silence, the pros and cons as to life, death, and his precious health, in going back across the Pass, or keeping on. We gathered about him and the Professor. I thought his talk a bit hypochondriacal; it bored me; that Jack might keep on only to escape the name of quitter. I resolved not to take his ailments too seriously, and went twice to the river for a drink, as he spun on.

"Here's another thing," he would keep beginning, "now I figure it this way," as to pains in your kidneys, snow, wading streams, and raft rope.

I suggested that the crowd vote whether he went on or back, to show our preferences, not to bind him. All said they wanted him to stay with us, though the Professor's arguments were for a return. He seemed anxious to hustle Jack off, while pretending great solicitude. Miller refused to vote, mistaking opinions for advice; saying, "It's a question Jack ought to settle for himself." Fred conditioned his vote by saying that Jack must never be left alone—while we're on the mountain, for instance—if he kept on. The Professor consented to let him have the Moth-eaten Bay, if he would return. Lucky for him he changed his mind; Fred and I were ready with a piece of ours if he hadn't, knowing how well life and death were at stake.

So, Jack decided to go back, after keeping us two hours, telling how he didn't want to delay us. Simon tried to skimp him on the sugar of his ten days' ration, and I delighted in making the kid double the amount. He wanted Jack to sign a statement that he'd left us voluntarily, which the Professor and I tabooed. That must be an Arctic wrinkle. Beside the skillet and the milk can, he took our spare axe, a baking-powder tin, and a cup. The adieux, as he packed the horse, were conventional.

And we have traveled twelve miles to this willow flat. A hot sirocco roars down the reddish mountains, swaying our drift-wood fire to singe your hair ten feet away, and chokes the beans with floury silt. In a gulch we passed the skeleton of Brooks' first played-out horse, the head lugged fifty yards away by bears; and right there the P.R. floundered feet-up, and was chopped out.

To-day's verse was original, suggested by Simon's repeating the Willie-and-the-Poisoned-Tea rhyme; and by Jack's departing:

> Three argonauts went North for gold,
> Starvation came; Jim died of cold.
> Said Jack to Bob in merriment,
> "Let's eat, and have more room in the tent."

No one seems to miss Jack much. His name hasn't been mentioned. That rabbit stew was great.

CHAPTER XI

RED FLESH FOR KINGS OF FRANCE

AUGUST 2.—We have crossed the entire range.

On to-day's "march," as the Professor always says, as if we had a brass band and a drum major, we left the Kuskokwim, for the mountains suddenly ended. We turned northeast to travel the last hundred and fifty miles to McKinley, in air line along the face of the Alaskan range. We jumped from silty woods straight into swamp, for as long as Brooks follows Herron (who kept on down river to get lost) the trail is dry, but Brooks traveling on his own hook always jumps neck-deep into muck.

Miller and I have just climbed the mountain over camp, which stands like a sentinel guarding the vast Kuskokwim valley. Up, up, but not once a foothold to stand upright, through knee-deep moss, avalanche-torn spruces, choking alders, and a big glacier-borne bowlder a thousand feet above camp—we reached aweing talus slopes, fringed with jagged cliffs. The sub-arctic's months of unbroken sunlight create the same endless, treeless rock fields that you see the year round on great peaks near the equator. The knife-like summit was like a breaking wave, yet with fragile Arctic poppies, defiant and abnormal, abloom on its crest. North, a dull, whitish network of bars and channels, a Kuskokwim tributary which we'll cross to-morrow, twisted on fans of fresh alluvium from out these endless, angular peaks of terra cotta. Northward drowsed the gentle foot-hill country, one rounded dome standing out mutely to lead us on.

But the west! There the wilderness unfolded, vast and dumb. There low, translucent mountains hovered far beyond the horizon, across some aqueous gap. Over all the great Kuskokwim was sprent a long-drawn lacework of crackly glass bits, dazzling in the eight o'clock sun. Ghostly shadows filled the low ridges and flat hollows of this no-man's waste, burned and naked, dull carmine with fireweed. Never was wilderness so silent and serene, so without inspiration, without even melancholy; so powerful, so subtle, so unplanetary. The barometer, "made in Germany," from the junk-box registered 26.5. And from the summit we saw, too, the acute angle made by the Professor's knees with his legs, as he stood by his tent far below, and Simon eating fruit—eating, eating—out of a tin cup.

AUGUST 3.—The Professor and I clashed again to-day. He never knows where he wants to stop on the trail. He's a fearful combina-tion of stubbornness and indecision. Long ago, he said that he ex-pected and wanted criticism, but no one dares advise or suggest anything now; but may laugh in his blue shirt sleeve, instead, at some of his moves.

This morning, as the others loafed in camp, Fred and I as usual hunted lost horses over miles of tundra and started tired. The Pro-fessor said that we should noon at the first river-fording. We cross all the streams draining the face of the range at right angles now. Horse-feed aplenty and water were at the river, but the Professor kept on a mile to where there was neither. As we chewed our dry bread, I said, "This is quite the cleverest thing we've done yet." "Where was there water and horse-feed last?" he asked quickly. "Right at the river," I said. He paused. "In using that word *clever,* I think you are going quite beyond your bounds," he said, and the crowd stared, as if a dynamite fuse were discovered fizzling out under their noses. I forbore. The idea of taking my remark seriously! He should have laughed, "If you want water, go back to the river and get some for all of us."

Nevertheless, I'm still suffering from the inevitable restraint this sort of foolishness gives. It may all seem a small matter, but in this life it's big as holocaust or battle in civilization. And this is only our second tiff in this lifetime of the storm and stress of travel, of *ego* galling *ego*. There's more laughter in a day than spleen. "Those are the things I try to forget," said Simon, when I told him I had recorded our fight. Yes, but the pleasant things will be remembered anyhow; the unpleasant are nearer truth as it is in this wilderness life, nearer the blessed weaknesses which make us human, which for some false pride the returning traveler suppresses.

Late this afternoon, we touched tree line again. In the moss lay the whitened saddle of the second horse of Brooks' to play out. Simon pounced on it and packed it along, girths and all. "He's got stuff enough there to start a pushcart," chuckled Miller.... "Cheap! Cheap!" went a wise picket-pin, sitting on a mound near by.

We're camped on white moss sloping to the north; on the left a creek and spruce, on the right a red mountain; ahead, forest mixed with ponds, the foot-hills unfolding beyond in the first quiet, cloudless twilight for weeks. The horse-bell is clanging hungrily in a bank of almost Keechatna red-top. We've eaten four prairie chicken shot by King, ahead of the pack train.

The Professor has spread a handkerchief over the back of his neck, because 2-mosquitoes-2 have been sighted, and is a sketch, making some sort of observation and scratching a bite at the same time. Simon, who is lying on his back, dead to the world, making gulping noises with his bread and tea, was called down for one of his favorite tricks to-day. The Professor saw the wood-and-leather lunch box (some scientific case of his, I think, which now is always tied insecurely on Bridget's pack,) full of finger-squeezed biscuits insides going to waste, thrown away by fastidious Simon. After sup-per, I found one of these hidden on the end of a log. I put it in plain sight on the moss. Simon came along, and when he thought I wasn't looking, stealthily threw the bread off into the brush—which is the kid to a T.

And we have only four sacks of flour left. The summer isn't half over, and a sack lasts only one week. We've hardly seen McKinley. What, besides pemmican, will we eat on it? As we've come in—and we couldn't get out that way much faster—we're more than four weeks' steady travel from the coast. Why don't we worry? Our stom-achs are always full, I guess, though only with beans. That's why.

We have counted on "living off the country," which no prospec-tor will ever do, because of Fred's tales how last year these foot-hills were alive with caribou, moose, and bear. But except the old grizzly and cubs a month ago, and the sheep on Tateno River, not a bit of blood-red meat have we seen. And both quarries our bum guns lost. "I don't see what good it 'ud do us *to* see a caribou," says Fred. "Couldn't hit one with that old .44 of the Professor's. Like some of them horses, it was a good gun oncet.... Yes, sir, las' year the caribou was thick on these hills. Must hev all migrated off. Yer can't tell in a big country like this. It's spotted. Game's here one year, there the next. I b'lieve the caribou has all took to the woods for winter, and we shan't see none without we stop to hunt."

AUGUST 4.—We struggled among the ponds, crossed a river, and toiled through burned forest, where smouldering fire gnawed the moss, and black bark scaled from the spruces as if by disease. Bare, dead roots rose gnarled and sinewy from the brick-red sand, as skin might decay and powder, revealing the bones of a corpse. Suddenly I saw a tawny form swinging in the open a-top a ridge, and signaled to Fred, who dashed ahead with the old .44, twisting his neck to see the beast, running in circles like a man with epilepsy. We halted the train, whispering, "Moose!" But soon Fred reappeared ahead cursing the gun, swearing he'd never use it again, even if a caribou poked him in the shoulder. He had only wounded a big grizzly lying on his stomach digging for picket-pins, who rolled over and made off solemnly into the woods. "And I ain't following no wounded grizzlies, not to-day," he added, "nor termorrow with thet old Winchester."

We covered rolling opens of white moss, where blue-bells, forget-me-nots, and white blossoms with coarse, aromatic leaves stood between lush banks of red-top and late snow-drifts. Bordering gullies of brown stones flat as a pounded pavement, where a drift had lately melted, willow and buckbrush would be planed off even with the general level by blizzard and cold, as if with a scythe, and lift atrophied twigs toward a sickly pond....

Out over the dumb valley, all day translucent clouds have glowed, produced anon and anon by mirage and obliterated; thin lines of hills, now intense purple, now like wasted, shadowy rainbows far below down there, changing deep emerald at twilight, foreshortened into a single line, yet shading the darkening expanse, whence you get some hint of a loneliness yet unknown to man, perhaps of suffering.

Again we camp in a clump of rotting cottonwoods, which always outlast spruce toward the mountains. I have shaved, I even brushed my teeth. Then Miller went me one better, and carried out his threat to bathe in the creek. But I surpassed him by giving my feet a soap wash. Somehow I never have time to take off and dry my socks.

AUGUST 5.—Fresh meat at last, though only a grizzly!

In the cold rain, we sighted a blur moving across the hills. "Moose!" again we whispered, and the train halted. Fred dashed over the ridge; a shot; a great, grayish beast with branching antlers, running—floating, rather—toward the mountains, turning now and then to stare at us through the fusillade. "Caribou," we breathed, seeing its white rear, though "Moose, moose," insisted the Professor.

Over the hills it leaped, down the slope, paused in the willows, pranced off up the talus, and over the ridge. I headed it around a hill into a creek bottom; King saw and tore down, but it nosed through the willows to more peppering—from the .44 nevertheless—and scudded into the horizon. What can you expect from that old Antarctic blunderbuss—and the Professor's initials carved on the handle?

We moved on, weary, hungry, cold, and wet. But in an hour we found Fred, who had followed the quarry into the horizon, standing by a brown, dead thing, a year-old girl-grizzly, caught unawares pawing vindictively for gophers. We unpacked for bags and knives, skun her for the back fat, dissected her innards and captured her liver. And I, for one, cut strips of warm flesh from the disembowelment, and ate them raw.

And to-night King had a go at the Professor. Fred wanted to camp in a cottonwood grove in mid-afternoon, our leader to go on. On we went. "We'll burn moss if we can't find wood," said he. "Then you'll have to cook supper over it," said I. You could as well burn snow as this rain-soaked sphagnum. But we found other cottonwoods, at last. Nearly all the horses went down together through the crumbling sod of the bank we climbed to camp; wedged themselves, lying on their necks and waving legs in the air turning back-somersaults, packs under them, tie-ropes choking them. The Dark Gray nearly kicked me silly, flinging his hoofs turtle-fashion, as I pushed him over on his side. Fred and I alone hauled, and tugged, and drove, for Simon and the Professor had welched up to camp. Fred was furious. He climbed the bank and shouted, "You evidently don't want no pack train any more. You don't never pay any attention to it." The two of them didn't budge; and somehow we managed to right the beasts, and hew a new trail up the slope.

But sudden sunshine and the meat humored us. First we ate the liver, which has the odor of smelts and is too sweet. After, King and I started up the glacier stream to find a crossable ridge for the train to-morrow, into the foot-hills, which are growing higher. We trudged up roaring willow-flats, with right at hand the pillars of two glorious rainbows, then around a greenish mountain on which rock, like bunches of dough, was stuck all over the talus. Head winds knifed us, clouds poured over a flat peak slashed with snowy gullies that quivered through the scud, as it were a wall dripping with tallow. We found Brooks' horse-tracks (we packers, always traveling with an eye peeled on the ground, can find horse-tracks wherever and whenever we want to) and climbed an easy ridge by a lush gulley filled with pie-plant, blue-bells, and forget-me-nots. And up there was a sheep, staring at us from a cliff ahead! Up we sneaked. He was an old ram, lying down resting his twisted brown horns with a bothered expression on his face, and his legs folded under him. We dropped, and crept on; but when next we raised our heads, and near five hundred feet higher, there scampered the old fellow's harem, a string of snowballs rolling up a summit two miles away. "Now ef a man was really starving," philosophized King, "he could put in a day, and git one o' them old rams."

So we've come back to a supper of dried apricots. Every twig and branch hanging over the fire is alive with wet socks. Simon has sewed on his black velvet cap a canvas visor made from the old saddle he found, and with his thin Mosaic whiskers, looks as if he was just off the yacht from Kishinev. Now he's patching his busted rubber shoe with what was left over from the cap. He's pitched the tent in such a holey place, King is sleeping outside. I hate the smell of punky cottonwood.

AUGUST 6.—We hit over the sheep ridge, and all day plunged dizzily down and up, over slidy talus cut with crags, through airy abysses, across little streams. The train slid and floundered, mashing feet, always out of plumb and off balance; and the Professor got nervous. You'll never believe till you see, how horses can be herded in such treacherous steep places, sometimes with a 400-foot cliff right under your own sheer slope. Bless the mean, tough cayuse!

> The King of France with twenty-thousand men
> Marched up a hill, and then marched down again!

New worlds of higher peaks, freshly snow-powdered, opened near, slid-to everywhere. "Good practice for McKinley," gasped the Professor on each summit, having always seemed to rest on the ascent at the wrong place, and for much too long.

We're camped at the forks of two small streams, in a courtyard of snow mountains and by poles of an ancient Siwash camp. Bleached sheep horns lie on the stones of an old fire;—yet nothing to burn but green willows. The Professor has trimmed his whiskers, and now resembles a codfish. He's lying on his stomach, studying the map with a piece of straw, to find how we're going to cover three thousand miles an hour, on a sled to be built some day, which he's always mentioning, to slide down from the top of McKinley. Miller threatens to wash again.

AUGUST 7.—Forever King-of-Francing it, and—then our first caribou.

This morning, King wanted Simon's Colt automatic, sacred to Simon, to stalk bear. Simon's excuse for hogging it—though he couldn't hit a glacier from its moraine—was that all the cartridges were packed on a horse. So, seeing a bear near a big river, instinct overcame Fred's oath never to use the Antarctic blunderbuss again, and off he dashed with it. Volley after volley echoed from the old iron, but Mrs. B'ar and her one overgrown cub loped away downstream and up a bank, stopping to peek at us now and then from the willows, and say, "What sort of a noisy gilly have we here, my child?" King came back cursing. The Professor still wouldn't admit that the gun was useless, and made uncovert hints that Fred had buck fever. But *he* will never shoot. Chewing stale bread in a broad glacier valley at noon, I diplomatically wheedled the Colt from Simon, and insisted on unpacking horses—all, if necessary—till we found cartridges. At that the Professor growled, till we told him that as Simon ran it that gun might as well be a walking-stick. Cartridges were in the second pack.

Instantly a caribou came nosing up a river-bar, edging toward us, advancing, retreating, in short swinging little runs, sniffing us nervously, nosing the air, as if punching holes in it. It's wonderful how they glide, keen head and delicate horns erect, in that thrilling grace of limb over silt and tundra, where we struggle. He saw us, paused, advanced slowly across the bowlders to investigate, with a "*Tsuss! Tsuss!*" like steam escaping from a valve. Fred fired the Colt. The creature ran back a little, pausing now and then to throw a puzzled look over his shoulder and say (to himself), "Now, what did you make that funny sound with?" He shook with sudden tremors, perhaps from a bullet, perhaps from mosquitoes, and loped far away. But in five minutes, another came bobbing and swinging up the bar, to within ten yards, as Miller calmly photographed him. Fred knelt, Simon hopping at his shoulder, whispering, "Lemme, lemme, oh lemme!" Fred fired. Fired again—again. The caribou shook himself, turned his back; slowly, slowly his front legs quaked, his fragile head went down, and up and down, as the Professor to vindicate the blunderbuss blazed away, too.

We sloshed across the channel to revel in the liver, blood, and entrails. It seemed to matter nothing that we had something beside fetid grizzly meat; paramount was—though plain to all but the Professor—whose shot had killed? A grand pow-wow over that began, all of us elbow-deep in blood, feeling for bullets. Fred at last found a .44, but only in the deer's neck. Thus the Professor's gun was vindicated, and Fred discredited with buck fever, and all on a scratch shot!

Now caribou are circling around camp; one browsing in a meadow, one beautifully reticulated with black horns still in the velvet against the sunset. They've investigated, and decided we're not worth while. For curiosity, they're quite beyond cats and women. Down the valley, ten sheep are crossing a talus to watch us cook; up, Miller is stalking four that impertinently peeked right into the green willow camp-fire. The mountains are netted with their paths, but stalk as you will, an old ram guards the herd, and it's off, leaping gorges, mounting sheer cliffs to three miles away and two thousand feet above at the first shot. They're very funny when they run—just white ermine specks against the vast talus, a string of snowballs, on invisible legs, pitter-pattering with an easy, sideway swing from crag to crag, and never a sound below down here.

So we're all happy, full of blood and fibrin; even Miller. His stomach had turned, like the worm of history, at fishy bear meat. Cold caribou grease is good as butter. Simon finds it better than sugar. He's even thrown away the two-inch bear steak he saved when we shot the caribou, and had said, "I may not like caribou as well."

AUGUST 8.—Angular ochre peaks feebly grassed and a bit too theatric as they vanish suddenly into calm snows; now and then a hanging glacier; scented fields of wild chrysanthemum deliciously crushed by the horses; gnarled streams and gravels in a bleak valley—eight hours we beat the brutes up two thousand feet, down two thousand; again, again, and again, ever northeast toward McKinley, a mountain ascent every half hour. "G——! I ken see Seattle," says Fred on a summit. "Let's go to the dance to-night. I hear Tom Healey's git a new pornograph in his bar. See yonder, they're buildin' on the new brewery. Hear there's been a strike. Getting home to-night, we'll ask thet whiskered old feller that comes in on the six-thirty train how the new court-house is comin' on down ter Skomockaway." A caribou played detective on us in each canyon, and one peeked over a bench at us as we ate at noon.

Toward four, we took a high saddle, and sliding down to Ton-zona River, got stuck on a craggy pinnacle. The beasts tumbled and coasted with the shale, bracing their four legs at once, scuttling down like peas over a gable, as we tore about crazily hallooing and beating them into line. Here from camp, in the first spruce seen for days, we're gazing up at that rock steeple, wondering how any horse—or man, for that matter—could have fallen from it without somersaulting in mid-air.

A fat bull moose, skulking a hundred yards off in the brush, wel-comed us here. Simon wanted to shoot him, but was suppressed. We can't carry any more meat, and who knows what prospector's life this beast or his offspring may not some day save? Alaska belongs to the free miner and Heaven knows Nature has given him little enough help in his fight against her. I am glad we've no murderous sportsman in the crowd.... Mr. Moose watched us awhile with a bored expression, like a prize bull in his pen at a county fair, and made a solemn exit up the mountains, as if to say, "Now, who do you think those busy freaks are? They annoy me." His dignity was rather travestied by a two-foot-long dewlap, which bobbed and swayed as he lumbered off. Bears "galumph," moose "lumber," you observe, and caribou, which are the most human, fascinating be-ings, "float."

Out on the gravel flat, we've been rendering out caribou lard from intestinal fat. As for me, I'm beginning to smell like a New En-gland farm-house. And Miller has washed again!

August 9.—Crossing Tonzona River to-day, our thousand-and-first Rubicon, all the horses were stoned into the vicious black water, tearing through drift-piles and wrecked spruces, wetting their packs. We mounted a bench to—desert. Bare, bleak, and vast, it stretched out as dumb as in the recent hour when its ice-cap shriveled; strewn with white granite bowlders, as if hurled there only yesterday from invisible cannon. Northeast we filed in silence.

"The beasts coasted with the shale, bracing their legs as we tore about ballooing and beating them into line." (Traveling through the foot-hill country.)

Smoke softened and made magical the unresponsive plain, recalling Whymper on the arenal of Ecuador, early rangers in the Rockies, trekking Boers, Napoleon back-trailing from Moscow. Far below its immensity, the stark forest brooded, pale purple, and beyond, a wasted carmine, like summer midnight in the Arctic. Eastward, stupendous peaks reared snows veiled in opal cloud and magnified by refraction. Over the highest, a pale blue nimbus shed watery rays of a million hues, down among ringed, azure snow squalls—the Dorean vision of a sunlit paradise.

I fell behind with Miller, and talking politics! Now and then a larger bowlder notched the smoky blue-pink horizon; always gigantic, though miles away. We crossed a dry stream of round, white bowlders, like an avenue of skulls, each splashed grewsomely with pink lichen—and Simon found a new flower. We passed a grassless lake. At last came a roar, like a mill-race pounding over iron arches, and two dusky miles betrayed a clump of Childe Roland willows, beside another path of skulls....

Caribou supper is over, and Fred, as usual, is changing his socks. He has three pairs in commission at once; one he sleeps on to dry them—which takes more courage than I should have; two are hanging on the reflector to improve the bread. Every morning, just as we pull out, some one rescues a forgotten fourth pair from a distant bush.

...Fred always finishes eating first. To-night, the Professor remarked that he was off his feed. "A hog eats fast, y' know," drawled Fred, "and don't take no small bites."

CHAPTER XII

UNDER THE SMILING SNOW

AUGUST 10.—We're traveling fast—near twenty miles a day—speeding down the last lap to McKinley.

To-day, broken ridges and brush corrupted the desert, and at noon we crossed the streams of a big brown glacier from invisible Mount Russell. We popped futilely at a dozen caribou in their huge bed of yellowed grass and pea-vines, as they flitted toward the notched morainal hills—grotesque and unstable there, under low clouds, hiding a queer gap in the great range....

S-t-u-u-u-n-g! "Zzz-whoo-op!" buzzed a wasp from my feet, as I batted Whiteface across a creek; and executing a parabola, got in his stinger between my eyes. The pain almost sickened me. Miller burst out laughing. "Your face looks like the fat boy's in Pickwick," said he. I could *see* my swollen cheeks. They felt like a couple of boxing gloves hung from my forehead. Oh, it's a great joke. The crowd thought it very funny, to halt the train, and photograph me. Soon, I couldn't see light out of my left eye....

Again we sleep on gravel. I've been digging out a sleeping hole to fit my hips, with the geological hammer; not many beds, I bet, are made that way. We boiled raisins for supper, Simon sitting rooted by the fire, drying a sock, unable to keep his eyes off the pot. It's clearing, if a right eye can see the truth all by itself. Clean, inky foot-hills of slate, veined with quartz, sweep down to our shadowy desert.

AUGUST 11.—Left eye was shut tight as a rat trap at breakfast, and the right was so bad that the Professor had to hand me my food and spoon. "How many sacks of flour are there now, Professor?" burbled Simon. I tipped off Miller and Fred not to speak up. "I have not looked up the matter lately," he sighed wearily, "but I presume about half are unused." "Half" would be five. We have two.

I stumbled about hunting horses, spite of the blindness, while Fred showed his first peevishness on the trip. "I don't see how we ken be sure of gitting more caribou, and we need the meat," he grumbled. "I b'lieve they're all high up, hitting the streams toward the mountains, an' don't see how we'll shoot more without we stop and hunt." And he growled on about "packin' up jest so each morning," and over the shortness of flour.

So to-day's adventure of the moose made Fred hot. One old mastodon peered at us at noon as we chewed our rubbery biscuit stained red from the leather in the box strapped on the Roan, and he vanished before any one could swallow and exclaim. Later, another thrilled the scrub willows as the Professor squatted to eat blueberries in a swamp. King stalked from behind alders; Simon, who couldn't see an elephant at fifty yards, snooped behind in his footsteps, with the .22, which made Fred sore. Shots and shots; nice horns shaking the willows, as the beast runs and faces jerkily about; bobs into a big clump for good. No more shots. Soon we move on. Across a creek, Fred was nosing the grass, which was bloody, and swearing he'd wounded the beast, which must be dead three hundred yards off. We need the meat. Of course, a hunt through the brush was on? Not on your life. I started for the ridge half a mile away, but the Professor moved on the train, shouting, "Follow!" to

Miller, who pretended not to hear; and Fred wouldn't budge from his blood trail, till the horses had vanished some time, and we had to quit. "It's only crazy men will kill a moose, an' then not stop to git him," burst out Fred between his teeth, "when grub's this low." Yes, if ever we're really short, d'ye think we won't rise and visit on the Professor this deliberate waste of half a ton of meat?

Yet soon Mount Foraker flashed forth over the clean, coal-black peaks, under a momentary sun, smashing in its white blaze and glint all concepts of magnificence. And then you saw it was only a Titanic, white-washed tree-stump, the segment of a mountain dropped from the moon. Such sights still disturb me. I ought to be old enough to understand them with better poise....

We're camped in spruce on a dry slew of Foraker's Herron glacier, named by Brooks for the Captain, who discovered the mountain—a perfunctory compliment between the Survey and its rival War Department. King, Miller, and I, in a grumbling, wonder-how-we're-going-to-get-out-of-the-country mood, climbed its acres of gravel-dump moraine, whence Fred seriously showed us how he could "git to her old summit in four hours. Yes, sir." Huge bowlders, ready to tumble at a glance from devilish Nature, hung on the sides of this wilderness of conical, even-heighted white mounds. Stark, naked, and transitory, Nature here overreaches herself from sublimity into hideousness, and all the repulsive elements of fear. If there's a hand of God, it's been more apoplectic on that moraine than when it blotted Pompeii or St. Pierre. Why? What *purpose,* right or vengeful, does such distortion fulfill? A green pond in a conical cup, walled by the moats of frozen gravel, casts glossy Foraker downward. The same crimson cloud that flatters its chill cap three linear miles above, fleecily spreads into the calm, solemn sunset of these grave-yard depths. A mouse runs through a sad fringe of grass. Below, the pothole where the river is born vomits a brown-white cataract, with the roar of steel girders being riveted, the color and thickness of canned evaporated cream.

We follow down the scarred bed of white moss, of bowlders reddened as with blood, of scarlet berries on mean bushes. In the woods a big caribou whisks about fifty feet away, snuffs, punctures the air with his nose; patters off a-snuffing. And at camp, Simon, having eaten three cups of sugar and fruit, ladles us a half cup each.

AUGUST 12.—Packed at last, and roaring through the Herron ice-stream, a herd of thirty little caribou, prancing and waving neat horns, met us as the goats in the Norwegian fairy-tale met the troll. Simon, asking what they were at thirty yards, dropped the Big Gray's rope in the river, so he bolted and scattered them. A lone dozen escaped in a willow slew, scampered up-stream toward the rest, and our mighty arsenal blazed away. One thin three-year-old fell. I avoided the butchering. I don't mind gutting a bear, but caribou are too human and gentle. Believe I'd only skin one if I were starving.

Then every hour was livened by caribou. Distant specks moved over the hills, herds of twenty-five and thirty fauns gliding to and fro, from snow to starker forest, out over this plain, which has not yet answered me, even with its melancholy. We halted, aimed at forty yards, and all shots went wild. "Chhoff!" they said, capering away in circles. Fred would gloomily presuppose us short of grub, without steaks, "three quarters lean, one quarter fat," as he says. One beast fell to the Colt on the stony ridge between two more glaciers, Simon grabbing the gun and plugging away after the poor thing was well dead. Blood was gurgling from the windpipe as I came up; Miller was cutting out his tongue, and the Professor photographing the creature. Simon loves to gut 'em. "I git him," said Fred, "right where I seen a big grizzly las' year, so I come there, thinkin' he might be settin' here yet."

We're camped in a slit in the bare glacier bench, a mile away from spruce. "May I ask why we've come up here, near no wood or water?" said I to the Professor. (Of course, we were going to try his magnificent experiment of baking bread with the fuzzy white tundra moss?) "Oh, there's water here, but your eyes are too swollen to see it," answered he. "By ——, my head isn't, anyway," I retorted, foolishly and angrily. Our third brush, or fourth, which?

I'm thinking of all the wonderful things I'll do when we get to the base of McKinley, which should be to-morrow; shave, brush my teeth, change the drawers I've worn for six weeks, mend my sweater, cut my toe-nails—

AUGUST 13.—Fate gave us luck, to get lost and so not reach the base on the thirteenth with thirteen horses. Two earthquakes bumped us at breakfast. In dense clouds we hit northwest up a gulch—the wrong one, I observed to Miller, but no one else would listen; up northeast, even east, and quite 2,000 feet; then north, northwest, west—in circles, of course, and soon downward. Came out below the ragged cloud-edge. There were the snarled threads of a familiar glacier stream, glinting the azure of clearing! King and the Professor stared vacantly. I bet them it was the same river we'd camped on. "Oh, we've gone further than you think," the Professor deceived himself. "Give you a two hour start traveling the way we came," said I, to Fred, "and I'll beat you back to camp." No takers. We wound out upon the flat tundra, and you could have put a rifle ball into last night's camp!

Fred and the Professor walked north alone awhile, twisting their necks; then led us straight away from the mountains and over all the highest moraines. "Now let's try going toward McKinley," said I, "by skirting the foot-hills." "Go over there alone, if you want," said King. "You'll follow," said I. In all this beef, one man said little: the Professor; seeming to put getting found again up to King. He decided at last to strike for a spur of the hills visible five miles off, as a caribou tripped and capered after us. Skirting a pond, Fred had even announced (but took it back later) that he saw his last year's horse marks. You can't fool a Rocky mountain packer, oh, no!

Camp's in the hollow of another glacier stream. "I believe it's a put up job between Fred and the Almighty not to get to McKinley on the thirteenth," says Miller. Simon is sitting alone by the fire, waiting to snoop into the raisin sack, I suspect, when we're asleep. All day the Professor, with a wink, asked him to shoot ptarmigan with the .22. At each flock the horses would halt, and Simon would make fat little rushes at the birds, but in the wrong direction, or they'd fly up from under him when his back was turned, till Miller and I died of laughing. Fred took his girl's gun at last and shot six. So we've been eating chicken stew. My socks are soaking in the brook—I hope below where we get cooking water. It rains so much I'm getting moldy.

AUGUST 14.—The congregation will please sing, "Nearer, My God, to Thee." We're here, where Brooks camped at the foot of McKinley, northwest face at the head of Tatlathna River, altitude 2,600 feet, fourteen miles as the blow-fly flies from its summit, after forty-six days' incessant travel—ten faster than Brooks.

Leaving camp, we hit straight to a mountain-top; down, and straight up to another—an exasperating way Fred has, instead of following the connecting ridge, which would be easier and thus shorter. Still it drizzled, but suddenly I began to fear for myself once more. There *was* McKinley. Falling mists defined a blur in mid-air; a white, feathery dome, tiny specks of rock and ridge lines developed, threw out the long, curved summit in breathless and suppressed proportion—sheer on its broad face, buttressed by tremendous white haunches to right and left, which quaked and quivered through the mist, mounting 20,300 feet, to the very zenith. Thank God that the speechless tundra was hidden!

Down in a stream lay two fat caribou; ours in two shots from the .44, though Simon danced like a stage villain behind Fred as he sneaked up. Bridget became a dripping butcher shop. We crossed a low range of hills, and such a plain of dark granite bowlders and corpse-white moss opened as you may not see beyond Siberia. And bunch grass grew where each horse in turn took a friendly bite—"a saloon weinerwurst free lunch," said Miller, brandishing the Professor's ten-pound willow tent-pole, "for mountain use," carefully whittled last night. A distant stream or something creased the waste; Fred scared two black foxes into their hole; an hour, and we descended suddenly to the moldy flour sacks, roaring granite, and condensed milk water of Brooks' camp in the willows.

No one shouted, no one cheered. I only observed aloud—I talk too much and too loud—"The baking problem is easily solved, isn't it?" and pointed to a dark tongue of timber eating up the valley from the forbidden tundra. You see, all the pilot biscuits being crumbled and eaten, we shall have to manufacture in the reflector unfreezable dry flour stuff to eat on the ascent—"zwieback," says our Ethelbert with his Teutonic leanings.

He pulled a hair from Bridget's tail, and fitted it into his theodolite—or Abeny level, I can't tell the difference—and stole the summit of old McKinley for his waistcoat pocket.

I have hitched the meat alforguses to a cinch line tied to a willow, and thrown them where the foaming silt water outwashes a steam laundry.

AUGUST 15.—First, we performed duties of toilet long looked forward to. Then we sat around in the drizzly gloom with my binoculars, indicating "possible" ridges and glaciers of the 10,000-foot range which we find separates McKinley from this valley; each pointing out a ridge or glacier which the other thought was a certain other ridge or glacier. Of course, the main mountain towers over the front range. Then the Professor, still hitched to L.C., led Fred, to see how high on the front range it's possible to take horses, up the valley of the largest of its eight visible glaciers. Miller and I took three horses, flour and the reflector across the stream to timber, to bake the zwieback. Simon posted himself by the sugar. I was to bake ten reflectorfuls of biscuit, enough with tea and pemmican to last four men ten days, cut all in two and double bake to expel moisture. I never want that job again. It took two hours to find a stagnant puddle in the distant timber. We'd forgotten a mixing pan, and started to use the teapot; but that was no go, too deep, so you wrenched your wrist off in the dough. Miller took the B horse back to get a pot. Black clouds from the southwest scudded overhead, bringing rain and half a gale. In the wet and blow, it took just one spruce tree to bake a pan of bread. The rain ran down the roof of the reflector, dripping into the pan; it steamed incessantly; first the flames shot in one direction, then another, and once—oh, glorious testimonial—even collapsed the thing, bread and all, and *folded it up*. It was fierce, felling trees, dodging flames, mixing flour, keeping the baked bread and baking-powder under cover in that storm. Miller only brought the gold-pan (Simon was cooking beans in the pot), from which half the flour blew away in mixing, and the rest filled with sticks and spruce needles. The two hundred and fifty biscuits were done at five o'clock. Then the double baking. Each panful took three times as long to dry as to bake, while Miller—now and then resting under a tree as I cursed and sweated on—chopped sixteen logs to pack up on McKinley to our last camp under the snow. At half-past eight we headed back to the river, only half the double baking done.

That long drive across the tundra! The dumb valley has spoken to me at last. It began to clear—the lustrous night-clearing of the North. Slaty clouds quivered upon us from the south under a sky of oceanic azure, and over the cataleptic valley hung a fringe of red and golden sunlight, as it were the border of some Miltonian heaven. We struggled over the bowlders. Big Buck with his sore heels kept taking to the mossy woods from the canary-colored lichen and stones of the old stream bed. Now a peaked rock face, now an enchanted, glossy ridge of McKinley swam below here; now the dark sky was lit from that glint of unfathomable seas upon its walls. Forest and tundra brightened, as by some inner illumination. I began to think, and think, and think. Neither of us had spoken for a long time. This was a strange place, a strange hour, an unnatural quest. How did it all come about? Why am I here? What for? Who are these companions? Miller paused to point out the sky ahead. I turned. Behind there was a range of hills—hills created in the moment, it seemed, in amethyst and spinel, in beryl and the grays of dawn; and through and over them poured the rich deep light "of creation or of judgment"—so said some voice within me. "The forbidden tundra and the smiling snow," it said. "You are between them. Beware!" And apprehensions, recollections, a hundred answers, fantastic, common sense, grotesque, came to the questions aforesaid; romances, confessions, wills and testaments, undreamed of tales of death, triumph and transfiguration—between the forbidden tundra and the smiling snow.

Miller shouted in my ear. It was eleven o'clock. We had reached the river in the first autumn darkness. Its roar was terrific, and we had waded sudden channels bursting out over the tundra far from its bed. Across, camp was dark and silent. We made a cairn of the wood, and the scud hurried us back across that flooding desert, to bed under the last shrivelled spruces below the realms of the smiling snow.

It's my birthday eve. We've lopped the lower branches of our trees, and lie spoon-fashion on lumpy wet moss. I shall be split down the middle. The blankets are soaked. The spruces leak like fury. We're wet to the skin. The fire, built by pushing over dead trees—all are rotten at the roots—is dying. Flour, zwieback, and einback, are under our ponchos, the last in Simon's botany box, absorbing moisture to beat the cards.

CHAPTER XIII

BUTTING BLINDLY INTO STORM

AUGUST 16.—Not a wink all night. We divided the last caribou steak, and wrung water from our blankets to make tea, which Miller wouldn't drink as we had no sugar. But we felt cheerier. The raw dawn shifted weary glints on the dull blue glaciers of the front-range. "What to do," thought I, "but go on zwiebacking?" I did. Miller cut wood. The baking over, we chased twenty caribou that had peeked at us, and hit back for the river. The flood hadn't fallen, but was spreading out into a hundred channels, so we waded it to camp. King crossed on Big Buck to get the wood, and it was very funny to see him buck in mid-stream with Fred on his back, too—the animated old wood-pile.

Simon was lazing by the fire, protected from the scud by a willow thatch importantly called a "Fuegian wind-break" by the Professor. He ran at me with all kinds of tales how we could get up some glacier—the one visible from here with the serac of dirty ice-blocks, under the highest point of the front range. The strange sacks of "mountain stuff" which seemed such a useless burden on the trail, were open, and weird Arctic clothing was passed around. I have drawn a pair of red stockings, with tassels, two pair of Arctic socks (like mittens for the feet), hand mittens, a pair of grimy drawers, and one of the green eiderdown sleeping bags.

Now, we can't all wander about in the McKinley fogs. Some one of the five must stay to read the barometer at the base camp under the front range, whither we move to-morrow up this stream. The Shantung silk tent holds only four, and there aren't enough green sleeping-bags—weighing just four pounds each, unless wet—to go around. The Professor won't say who must stay behind, which seems to lie between Simon and Miller. I want Miller to climb, and told the Professor that it was a good deal to risk our lives with the kid, whose eyesight and hearing are defective, and is slower than old Ned. "Yes, Miller is more adaptable," was all he answered. Miller says he thinks that Simon has some previous agreement to be taken on the mountain; but I doubt that.

Now the Professor says that he expects "a man to volunteer to stay behind," which is the devil of a scheme. Yet vaguely he adds that whoever shows up worst on the first day's climb, goes back. Whew! How can such vacillation get our confidence? He's simply afraid, or unable, to decide anything beforehand. Of course, Simon has corraled a rucksack and a green sleeping-bag, and is importantly hammering the heads on the ice-axes. One he has already used to chop willows. Miller saw, and cursed him. I'm in the tent, mending those grimy drawers. The rest are out in that Fuegian wind-break. No one knows it's my birthday. What's the use?

AUGUST 17.—At bedtime last night the river was gouging away the bank so fast that Simon made a danger alarm by tying a rope to a log and hitching the end in the tent. We'd slept two hours, when the rope jerked. Outside, the stream was sweeping away that Fuegian business and splashing the grub. The Professor jumped up out of three inches of water (he's a sight when just awake, fingering his long, pale locks out of his eyes) and lugged the stuff dazedly into the brush. King wouldn't budge. "You never can tell with these glaysher streams," he drawled, and rolled over asleep. Miller turned in with me, and though I invited the Professor as well—perhaps too insistently—he wound himself up in his tent well out of the wet and in the morning was snoring there, like a big human chrysalis.

I chased and found the horses—King tracked them wrong for once—by the creek where we shot the last caribou, and we were packed and hiking up the south fork of our flooding stream by noon, as it rained again; the fifth incessant day, mind you. Near the moraine of the glacier the Professor had explored—and little enough had he seen in the drizzle—the fog shut down tight. Instead of steering on by compass, we camped, though grass still struggled through the moss, and we could not go wrong in that narrow gorge. Having nothing but bowlders to tie the horses to as we unpacked, Little Buck ran amuck, scattering sacks right and left, and stampeding the whole bunch.

Thus we enter the fog to attack the virgin peak of Mt. McKinley, unknown and unexplored from all sides. Thus, without proper reconnoitering, we have jammed our heads into the 10,000-foot range which walls the main mountain mass. It seems to curve, and join the right-hand, or south haunch of the main dome, whose face has appeared quite perpendicular. Below that face, between it and our outer range, and at right angles to our direction, flows Peters' glacier (named by Brooks). We think that it heads into a curving wall, connecting front range and main mountain, by which we hope to reach an arête of the peak. But so reticulated with ridges and hung with glaciers are these heights, that I doubt if any one of us has a clear idea of just where we are going to hit; or will have, till clear weather comes. This is our base camp, and we're ready to make a ten or twelve days' attack on the old mountain without descending. Yet August is the Alaska rainy season, and it may drizzle on till the September frosts, which will mean checkmate by fresh snows on the mountain.

The outlook is cheerless: we're discouraged; the low clouds rain on, and on, and on. Grub-packs and pack-covers are saturated. A spirit of "Oh, let it go, it's wet anyhow," pervades camp. The ground is littered with old boots, smelly sacks, unwashed dishes, and slabs of caribou which Fred has discarded after careful sniffs. Handfuls of fly-blows crust the meat bags.

Yet the Professor talks of pushing up the glacier anyhow, to-morrow. He has been out reconnoitering with King, and announces that he's found a way for horses across the moraine to the ice. I took a turn over the black hill which splits the ice-foot in twain, and we call the "nunatak." Saw nothing, nothing, but crazy cataracts of mud water, in crazier gorges.

AUGUST 18.—Wetter drizzle. I was annoyed, because he had talked of moving, to find the Professor asleep in his tent with Miller, after breakfast over the stone fire-cairn I had built to econ-omize wood; especially as he'd been trying to persuade King to go down the valley to hunt. King was in bed, too; so what for me but to turn in? We recited a few drummers' tales, and worked in a laugh over the querulous one beginning, "Father, pass the gentleman the butter"; when enter Simon, with a butter can full of roots, and spread his drying-frames all over our tent.

Fred and I cooked tea and meat outside alone. Simon says that the Professor was sore because we didn't call him to eat. "That was the first meal prepared on the whole trip," he had complained (but not to me), "to which we were not all called." Oh, dear! We're kept entirely in the dark about his plans; no one cares to make a sugges-tion or ask a question. But sometimes the manner of his silences lets the cat out of the bag. He has made no decisions yet, of any sort, whatsoever.

So here we lie abed soaked; listening to the roar of glacier streams, the rumble of snow avalanches, the sandy splutter of driz-zle on the saturated tent. Now and then we peek out and make a

great to-do if a bowlder more than ten yards off looms up. Then
says Fred bitterly, "It's a-goin' ter clear. Yes, sir, she's a-goin' ter
clear. See her, see her."

AUGUST 19.—And still rain. "Simon," said the Professor this
morning through the drizzle, "go down to the stream and read the
barometer" which meant that we were going to hit up the glacier.
Nothing was said about who should stay behind; still no one dares
ask the Professor his schemes. Fred, as we stumbled in the fog hunting horses, was very peevish over the shortness of grub, Simon as a
companion on the mountain, and the Professor's indecision, especially as to who goes on the ascent. "Perhaps he thinks I ain't clean
enough for his eidy-down," he said. All but he have sleeping bags,
yet he is treated as essential for the climb.

At last we found and packed with rucksacks, small kerosene cans,
Primus stove, etc.—and Simon's dunnage—Whiteface, Bridget,
B horse, and the two Grays. We breakfasted on meat tainted from
its mildewy sack and stewed in its absorbed water, and plunged upward into the fog toward the unknown ice. No one stayed behind.
Each led a beast; crossed, re-crossed over sharp bowlders, down
and up sheer, sliding talus, to stumble with feet and hoofs grueled
by bowlders hurtled along under the brown foam of glacier
streams. Finally over sharp moraine, like the Andes in miniature—
to a luminous smooth lip of foggy ice.

We started up. It grew suddenly steep. Big Gray stumbled and
fell, but was righted before rolling over. The ice whitened; leveled.
The horses nosed a few lateral crevasses, nickered, jumped them
with awkward care. Gradually, huge seracs (ice-falls) swam through
the lightening mist, and a castellated black ridge struck down to bi-
sect the glacier into two amphitheatres. The Professor turned into
the left hand and nearer one, against Fred's protest. From our futile
talks, I had got too hazy ideas of where we were aiming to speak up.
Between two upper seracs, fresh snow hid the crevasses, and the fog

thinned. The Professor went ahead, sounding with his ice-axe. It was slow, ticklish work, winding back and forth over cracks that might, or might not, let you through to wait for the last trump— you couldn't tell till you tested them. The horses snorted; balked; leaned back, legs quivering, till we beat a terrorized jump out of each. I had on sneakers, and was thinking what a testimonial could be made to the rubber company for wearing them to 7,000 feet on McKinley, when the Dark Gray bungled a leap, and lost his hind quarter down a crevasse. All hands unpacked him, and hauled him by saddle tie-ropes. Now and then the other beasts imitated him. Higher and higher we felt a way; piloting each horse in turn across each crevasse, quadrilling—at last over clean ice, netted with cracks—to a dome-like summit. Beyond, the glacier dipped down all around to vague ice-falls hanging upon paste-white walls banded with brown irony veins; and to the left and north, but not toward McKinley, a possible-to-climb talus slope flanked the dizzy ridge. The Professor drew a brass aneroid from his money belt, and muttered, "Seventy-five hundred feet."

Fred, Miller, and I, cramped in the silk tent, are trying to fill the oil stove to give the beans another boil. (Simon only half cooked them.) We are talking weather, ice, and glacial erosion. Under us are wet blankets, wetter tarpaulins, wettest ice. It is suffocating hot; disordered food, clothing, instruments, all are steaming. Outside, some attempt has been made to sort the stuff, but it's rather hopeless; pounds have been added to the rucksacks, and the sugar is syrup. The smell of meaty, mildewed cotton pervades the air. The Professor and Simon have gone out to reconnoitre the talus between the glaciers, following a route to shore (off the ice) explored by Fred and me, roped....

At supper, he and I shivered outside the tent, as cups of tea and chunks of caribou were handed out from low voices within here. The zwieback was voted a success. The Professor is going to use it at the North Pole. Now and then—as the clouds parted overhead to

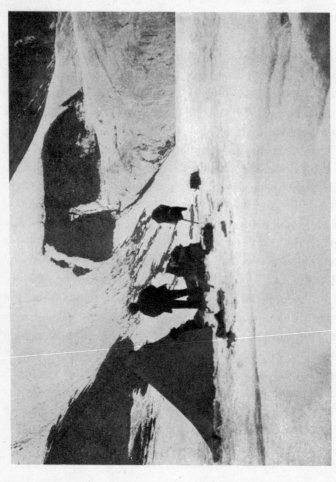

"Some attempt has been made to sort the stuff, but it's rather hopeless.... The real Alpine thing, this." (First camp on the "Front Range," Mt. McKinley, altitude 7,500 feet.)

let down a chill, silverish light, conceal the wavering edge of this snowy cistern, reveal shreds of sky too cold and lustrous to be blue—Fred would say, "Yes, sir, a hundred and sixty acres more of heaven cleared off. She looks like the break-up of a hard winter."

We're all five to sleep here to-night, some one outside, as the tent, being meant for one man, holds only four. Just now, Simon took our breaths away by volunteering, and is rigging up a sort of couch out on the glacier, like a funeral pyre, of sacks, blankets, and boxes. The tent is guyed down with ice-axes. We have one teaspoon among us. Yes, it's the real Alpine thing, this. Good night.

AUGUST 20.—The Professor and Simon climbed the ridge to 8,100 feet last night, reporting the outlook ahead through the fog "favorable" enough to try. All night I lay awake listening to avalanches, squeezed between Fred and the silk wall, mostly against the wall, which dribbled water till near morning, when everything froze stiff. Then the Professor struggled over on his stomach, fingered the pale locks out of his eyes, and started the stove at his head, for tea, zwieback, and caribou. No one washed. Outside, Fred and I rubbed snow on our faces. No use. We had no soap. When I had suggested we take some, the Professor laughed at me. Then we drew in our frozen boots from the outside—they're never allowed to touch the tarpaulin under us, as they import snow—and put them on gymnastically, one by one, as the others lay cramped and still as cataleptics.

Without, it was absolutely clear. Never were such steep walls, such hanging glaciers jeering at the laws of gravity, such over-brilliance of sunlight and azure sky. Above our amphitheatre, snow-slides had fingered straight converging paths down its mysterious east wall, upon the chaos of pale bowlders and yawning crevasse which surrounded us like a sea. Southwest, we looked out over sharp-angled black slate and rusty tuffa, clean cut and glistening as if created yesterday, to the foot-hills fronting the hidden

Foraker; and far below and away shone glacial ponds like diamonds strewn over the forbidden tundra. But clouds were gathering.

We were to climb the explored talus; curve around to its east wall; travel south, then east, around the headwall of the yet-unseen Peters glacier, to the south haunch of the main mountain. Slowly we packed our rucksacks, and double-tripped the outfit to "shore." Then each corraled what looked heaviest and was lightest, what according to suspicion as he read his neighbor's eyes overstated its weight—or understated it—if he thought anything was to be gained by ostentatious heroism. When all had forty pounds anyway, we found that another trip would have to be made up the ridge with alcohol, tent, and stove. I had the two two-pound cheeses, ten cans of milk, pea soup, and my clothing. Simon had the little olive oil cans of kerosene, and Miller the two twenty-pound tins of pemmican, that there should be no doubt about *his* pack. At this moment it was vaguely bruited that Miller was to take the horses back to camp to-night, no matter how high we climbed to-day, and read the barometer below while we are on the mountain. How this came about, I don't know. On top the ridge Miller tried to tell me, but couldn't make it clear. I gathered that the Professor's procrastination sort of froze him into offering to sacrifice himself. "It's pretty hard after all we've been through to miss the main chance," he told me. "I only wish that the Professor had let me know before hand I mightn't have a try at it." But Miller never kicked. Surely he hadn't "shown up worst," then. No one has had a chance, even yet. So the Simon infliction is a fact. Yet wouldn't Miller sooner than Simon shake hands with the danger devil before meeting him?

We began the ascent of Mt. McKinley.

Up shot the talus, straight as Jacob's ladder, into the clouds, and we hanging to it—Fred first, I last, and the rest strung in between. We kept now to rock-slide, to snow-slide, to glacier-edge. Heads bent to stomachs, sweating, gasping, we stopped to turn in silence every two hundred steps and view the poor horses, reduced to specks in their snowy purgatory, headed in on an island among crevasses—poor brutes that, twenty-four hours without food, had tried to find a way down to moss and lost their nerve. Fred kept tearing ahead, and made a point of always leaving a resting-place just as Simon and the Professor stopped there. Once the Professor, carrying the tent-pole, fell on a snow slope, and seemed nearly to roll to bottom. I caught Fred at the summit. He was leaning over an undercut snow cornice, dripping icy stalactites, God knows how many thousand feet, into the amphitheatre of glacier seven. A sickening look. We lay on our rucksacks, eating the last of the raisins, whose bag has sloughed away in the wet. The others grunted up to our side; Miller first.

Clouds had settled where the ridge mounted in the east. Thither the Professor, Fred, and I slabbed the talus, and sat down to wait for clearing—to wait, and wait, and wait. The base of the next rise lay across another cornice; to go down, then up to reach it, steps should be cut. I said that I'd follow anyone across, that way, or by the cornice. "No," said the Professor, "that won't be any use unless it clears. We must see where we are going." (Sic.) He went on to condemn the outlook into amphitheatre seven—"No possible slope from there, either," he said, "and even if we can get up this ridge to its peak, we are not sure of getting further." He did not see as far as this last night, he added. It seemed to me, that before butting up there we should have made sure of what lies behind this summit, if it took days; but I forbore to speak, and in such a place, that did not take much effort. Fred observed that horses properly shod could cross below the cornice. Still we waited. Behind, Simon in his poncho, like a fish-bone pen-wiper with his bow-legs, paced up and down like Napoleon before battle; and Miller, cold as usual, with his mackinaw collar turned up, was lying flat.

The Professor repeated, summarized, emphasized his objection to going on, and spoke of a return; but no move was made. And still no move. I suggested that we wait for it to clear until a certain moment, three o'clock say. It was so agreed, and on the moment we returned. The dilemma was restated to the others, who made no comment; and down the talus we slid, as the drizzle re-began, double-tripping the whole outfit across the crevasses, to where tea leaves, sodden in the ice, marked camp.

A catechism eked from the Professor that we should next try Fred's amphitheatre—the one to the east—which he had wanted to tackle. We saddled. Never were frozen hands so tortured on wetter, dripping cinches, galled in so inane defeat, on packs that were sponges. Back and down we have quadrilled over serac and softening snow-bridge, to camp on a quarter inch of gravel, covering water-flooded ice at the forks of the glacier. The horses savveyed the crevasses better; nosed and jumped them by instinct, in pathetic impatience at release, and when unpacked, tore away through the scud, down the lower reaches of the ice, leaving Simon and Miller in the lurch. Both return also to the barometer camp, to bring up fresh beasts to-morrow, unless it still storms. For this order, as affecting Simon, many thanks....

The sound of the horse-bell has just died. The drizzle is changing to snow. Again we're cramped in the tent on the sopping ice-gravel, playing detectives on ourselves and everything, to keep from touching the silk wall in the tiniest corner and making it leak. Under us, the sea-island cotton tarpaulin lets water through like tissue-paper. The Professor has just gone out to whirl a glass tube about his head—a thermometer, I think. He reports finer snowflakes. Every now and then we peek out under the flap, carefully lifting the soggy boots that keep it down and extend it. Of mountain ascents we don't say much. A snow-slide roars down somewhere, and Fred observes, "Another lumber wagon." Every now and then the Professor clears his throat. Nothing is said of our rebuff, or of the future....

Well, the caribou meat is stewed in the granite plate. The pea soup is slowly coming to a boil.

AUGUST 21.—Four inches of snow fell last night, and twice I unloaded the tent wall, which was pressing down and wetting us. I thought that the Professor would never grunt over and light the stove—but what was the use? You couldn't see the packsaddles in the fog ten feet from camp. Toward noon, Fred and I felt our way northeast up the glacier, rounding the hill of dirty ice-blocks, visible from so far down the valley. The Professor went exploring south, along the ridge leading evenly to the highest point of the front range, but condemned for its length and indirectness as a route to the supposed head of Peters glacier.

Unroped in the driving snow, King and I wound among the sheer crevasses of the serac, where you could look down from four to four thousand feet. We poked with ice-axes, crawled from little ridge to ridge of hard snow. We gained the foot of a col joining the ridge that bisected the glacier. It looked possible to climb; at least, everything else was perpendicular. We started, when out from the white gloom below, and refracted to a spiritual nearness, tinkled a horsebell. So Simon, afraid to be left behind, had brought up the horses despite the storm. We kept on harder; turning to the left around the spur, shinning the upper walls of crevasses where the glacier became almost hanging; higher, higher, till we topped the soiled snow-blocks, and steps had to be cut in the crevassed cliffs. More quadrilling to gain steep snow-bridges, and one huge crevasse where if you slipped you shot into the eternal like slush down a gable. I missed a jump on the first try, and slid back—a little. Towering ever above, swam the wall, now to waver to sheerness, now settling to a human angle, with the refractive trick of all snowy places even in clear weather in Alaska. So we plugged blindly on in the storm, where no foot had ever trod, up the scaffold of the highest peak on the continent.

Should we hit for the ridge's summit? Could more be proved from the top than from yesterday's height? Was this slope practicable for heavy packs? I was ardent, Fred apathetic. We kept on. The névé steepened, and we struck a rock gulley, lifting our bodies by our arms. Not a word spoke we. Vaguely we discerned the dark ice-blocks below, quivering deeper and deeper through the shaking flakes; vaguely the smooth slope, where the Professor had gone, arose and extended with us. Now treacherous, pasty granite pierced the snow. We'd stop to discuss if packs could be got up here. Now I was willing to return; but no, Fred had started, and must reach—somewhere. Two rock pinnacles, which had tantalized for an hour, neared into the likeness of those cliffs in Whymper's drawing of where old Humboldt met defeat on Chimborazo. We passed them. The coulée divided, and we came out upon a little nub of decaying granite. The storm seemed to thin. Light, like the first streak of winter dawn, settled upon the long ridge opposite. Suddenly, what we believed to be the top of our slope stretched itself a full thousand feet higher into the sky; and steeper, steeper. "Look, look!" I cried, and if the ridge had crumbled with us into the valley, we should have still stood staring.

That was enough for Fred. It was after four o'clock. Rock had ended. Sheer, hard névé, covered with six inches of fresh snow, down which balls were even now grooving trails, alone filled heaven. The aneroid said nine thousand feet. Fred crawled to the edge of the granite nub, to gaze straight down the most disturbing distance yet, into the abandoned amphitheatre of yesterday. When I look into such places, I have a feeling—not vertigo, not exactly fear, that worries me. I think too fast and too much, and of impulses which are not quite sane. So, down we slid, again defeated, Fred recklessly, I carefully bridging the crevasses; past the Humboldt cliffs, where the snow shut in denser than ever, and the long white ridge became a dark, magic line over the shadowy glacier.

Four horses were shivering on the gravel humps near camp. Miller was in the tent, making pea soup. From a distance, Simon and the Professor approached wearily. "We didn't think that you'd go so far," said the Professor, when we told that our ridge could be climbed, possibly with heavy packs. He paid little attention. "But you see," he discouraged, "even if it can, we don't know what's beyond. The problem is," etc., and he went on to tell how he and Simon had looked into a valley beyond the long ridge toward Mount Foraker, where the slopes were better, he said, and "we can get around to the main mountain on the divide between them"— (McKinley and Foraker, doubtless)—and where the rock was "much better, dark, apparently slate, and not that treacherous granite." Then he ordered to pack up and return the whole outfit down to the barometer camp!

Wondering how the weather could have allowed him to see so much in the next valley south, I protested mildly, "I hate to leave this place so soon and so suddenly." "So do I," he answered, "but what else is there to do?" And then recurred to me what I had left there in mid-air with Fred, that on a mountain of this size, unexplored, yet unseen in its entirety, it was foolish to stake all on a dash up one questionable pinnacle found blindly in a ten days' storm.

We started down to the valley—irony of ironies—as the snow clouds overhead boiled in the forgotten gold of sunset; and under a shreddy cloud-edge draping the glacier, the forbidden tundra, far as the eye could reach, shone clean and rosy....

Just now, after cleaning all the soggy food and stuff out of the large tent, and crawling into our steaming bags in the old comfortable way—feet on dunnage, heads on pants and sweater wrapped in poncho to extend the wall and get the drip—Simon made Fred and me very, very tired. "Well," said the kid, with most transparent bravado, "now I think that our chances for getting to the top of McKinley are brighter than ever. We'll get around to the south side of this glacier to-morrow, where the Professor explored, and we're practically certain of finding a good way to the summit of this front range."

Neither Fred nor I spoke. That sort of insincerity makes me boil. As if it would do any good in such a story-book, Arctic traveler–fashion, to *lie* in order to keep up our spirits. Pretty examples of courage men must be to rig up a fool's paradise around them to give them nerve. Victory lies first with whom best faces the darkest side of the picture, and fights upward from the worst. Wonder if Simon wasn't parroting the Professor.

CHAPTER XIV

REMORSE AND SALT

AUGUST 22.—To-day, dazing sunlight and ragged cloud revealed each disheartening detail of our valley, and countless more walls all quite perpendicular, netted with the converging paths of avalanches. Fred went wrong after the horses, Miller and I saw and chased them, down the glacier stream onto the now purple tundra, whence over the great gravel moraine all the slopes of the valley toward Foraker, peered into by the Professor yesterday, were laid bare. They astounded me. All were more impossible than the ridges abandoned. Thinking again of Simon's last night's "holler," as Fred calls it, I wondered had the Professor seen anything at all there. With Fred, we agreed that our only chance to reach the southwest shoulder of the summit dome was by following Peters glacier to its supposed head. "I always wanted to go there first," said Fred (but I don't remember that). The Peters ice flanks the actual face of the mountain, behind the front range; but about twenty miles northeast of us turns at right angles and flows straight out upon our tundra.

We told this plan to the Professor. He cleared his throat and said that first we should look into his Foraker valley from a hill downstream. The quick descent of five thousand feet has depressed us all physically, made us logy and headachy. We climbed this hill, browsing lazily on blueberries. Beyond rose another, and another; and though no more of his valley was to be seen than from back of camp, the Professor would go no farther to support his yesterday's enthusiasm. So silently, and quite out of caribou—though as we descended a big buck skipped from the willows at the glacier's gravel-foot and past Miller's nose—we faced for Peters....

Thus outwardly begins again only the old grind of packing across these vacant hills; but a suspicion distorts every moment of the day. So far, I hope this diary outlines the passions of exploration in moments of vivid struggle against nature at her worst, written down under their own stress; the thing as it was, at the time when it was—necessarily, and so the more humanly—with all the inevitable prejudices of personal equation. But now I seem to feel that the Professor is not trying his best to climb the mountain; that recognizing that it is beyond us, he is making half-hearted tries to escape our judging him a quitter. I know that I speak and growl quite as if I were sure of it. How unfair this may be, I hope is yet to be told in the supreme test of a final try; yet I think that events up to now justify my view, even from the standpoint of a return to civilization, with its viewpoint—ever served us by the explorer; ever poles away from any reality. Every member of the party, except me, has always spoken as if he thought that to reach the top of McKinley would be little harder than scaling—Pike's Peak, for instance. Simon has said that he judges from Herron's sketch of McKinley, made from a hundred miles away, which looks like a white potato. The Professor has declared oracularly that we should scale five thousand feet a day. Nothing could shake these opinions up to now, and doubts which I used to express were smiled on as mildly mutinous, though I alone of us have had experience on snow mountains in Alaska. If their confidence has only been a prop to determination, I hold it a pretty false, even cowardly frame of mind in which to approach a great task. If such self-deception is customary, as I gather from their talk that it is, on polar ventures, it is easy to understand all this constant failure in the far North. I started out strongly doubting that we could ascend McKinley, as many men of Alaskan and Alpine experience agreed, but determined only to make the hardest kind of a try.

Thus we have driven the train northeast over a big hill, to camp on a small, clear stream flowing from foot-hills at the middle of the front range. On top, Fred shot a caribou doe. Simon has scraped the hide, and tacked it to the moss with wooden pegs....

I have had to air my troubles to some one, and I knew Miller could be trusted; his voice is so low, anyhow, you never hear him. We climbed a hill to stare at McKinley, whose immensity grows into you, through you. We talked. I told him that I was angry with myself for having consented to come with these people, whose experience on snow mountains was nil—though God knows, mine is small enough. I felt guilty, that in my ardor to get back to my beloved Alaska at any cost, I had swept aside prudence and commonsense. I felt most foolish and simple-minded that I had not faced the issue squarely, but with deliberate blindness have swallowed all their precocious confidence. Lord! I could go on like this for pages, but I won't.

The Professor determines on a certain move; he has the feat accomplished before starting. He will not hear of difficulties, and when his unreasonable dream of success balks, or turns out a nightmare, he is all meekness and dependence, and asks your advice in a hopeless, demoralized way. When we turned back from this Foraker valley, I said again that I was sorry to leave the front range. "Why didn't you mention that before?" he reproached me. Thus my antagonism to him and all his ways increases. But I criticise him with no conceit that I could do better; I couldn't do as well with our equipment and personnel—I can't keep my temper, nor take anything in life, even reaching the summit of McKinley, with his placid, stubborn seriousness.

Miller said: "When I read about you all in the papers, I thought that you were experts at mountain climbing." He agreed with my worst suspicions about the Professor's not trying his best.

Returning, we saw the horses wandering down the tundra, and the Professor on an opposite hill, staring like a Memnon in the twilight at our unconquerable mountain.

AUGUST 23.—Sacred to the memory of Simon's botany box, slippery, unpackable thing, curse of the whole pack train and especially the P.R. Sorrel, who carried it. We cremated it after breakfast this morning. The epitaph:

> The botany box,
> Oh, the botany box!
> How many hard knocks
> Gets the botany box.
> We shower with rocks,
> And squeeze our old socks
> On the botany box,
> Oh, the botany box!

The Professor got up gumption to examine the now soggy zwieback stored in it. Having tried to dry in the reflector the bottom layer, which was mush, we ate half of it. Thus the box was superfluous. The rest we put into sacks, "to dry by ventilation," said the Professor. Simon even smiled at the funeral. Ere lighting the pyre, Miller photographed him, posing over his precious, outrageous treasure.

Last night the Professor came down his hill with a grand tale that the 12,000-foot ridge, running north from the main mass of McKinley, was broken, letting Peters glacier flow east into the Sushitna valley, not out upon our tundra, so that we cannot reach it without crossing the front range. None of us had noticed this. I climbed the Professor's hill before breakfast, and wasn't convinced.

After, he dragged Fred and me up there with him. Neither of us had his sharp eyes, so he sat down and talked observations with his "made in Germany" compass, which I copied into a little blank book. Thus Fred's and my blindness excused a reconnoissance. After a long rag-chew, the Professor decided to climb with me a peak at the point where I think that Peters, beyond it, bends toward the valley; we could see more from a higher snow peak near by, but the Professor seemed shy of exertion.

In the peculiar, deadening silence usual in his companionship, we two struck off at an angle from the pack-train and, dawdling along, watched it stop to play hide and seek with caribou, hear shots, see it move quickly on. At the foot of our mountain, he insisted on eating our fried caribou chunks before nine o'clock; and then fell in the most humorous manner into a crick you could spit across. We toiled up a long, monotonous ridge. Yards of fine talus near the top started sliding down with me, and I jumped to firm rock with an icy heart. You almost needed a board to sit on the 6,000-foot summit. From here, Peters plainly bent out toward our tundra (as indeed Brooks maps it); and though we could see above the bend no more than from camp, a break in the 12,000-foot, main north wall of McKinley, and so the Professor's suspicions were plain absurdities. He admitted this, for a wonder. The snow peak I had wanted to climb shut out any good view.

"Our first task is, therefore, to thoroughly explore Peters glacier," he said, "trying to find a more practicable route up the mountain." "And if we don't find one?" I asked. He coughed. "We will do all we can," he answered, "*in our short remaining time.*"

From that summit we picked out a camp for to-morrow on the opposite (north) side of the Peters ice, right at the bend under the 12,000-foot wall, on the last stream-netted talus of a dozen valleys meeting the lower reach of the glacier. I was for crossing yonder; burning to peek up the awful gap between McKinley and the fatal front range, sheer 5,000 feet on one side, 15,000 on the other; but the Professor wasn't, and sighed that we'd "see it all to-morrow," so we hit for camp. First we tried one arête down, which he pronounced too steep; then from another we glissaded over a long snow bank, to where a stream ran under the gray ice among Titanic cones and arches. We walked to the middle of the two-mile-wide glacier, now slipping over streaks of clear ice, now ankle-deep in muck, now toiling over rock moraine like Hedin's pictures of hummocks on the Gobi desert. The roar of streams came up louder through the gravelly ice, and surface trickles cut bowl-shaped meanders down. The Professor was bum at picking a way; he puts it up to you for a while, and then insists on changing the route, so I always swore, when he spoke, that it made no difference how we went. It was one of those endless, useless walks; the spruces below the moraine never, never showed, for we were on the wrong periphery of the glacier, which bowed slightly to the south. At last a rocky gulch, leading to cottonwoods.

Finally I broke silence. It came hard to make him discuss our rebuffs and chances on McKinley. He expressed the same blind confidence that we should reach the summit, but now it seemed tinged with melancholy. He concealed his doubts badly by a kind of smiling naïveté, which made his confidence ring even less sincere—and that sort of self-deception makes me furious. The momentary rasp in his throat, his precise phrasing, grated on my worn nerves; but I bore it quietly. At length, in a moment of real depression, he said, "Yes, I'm afraid it may be as Doctor —— said, that it will take two seasons to climb this mountain." I was, for once, all tact and sympathy, but it was like drawing teeth. Of course, failure would be more terrible for him than for me. In my selfishness, I had never thought of that, till this real flash of doubt bared the poor man's heart. At the end, I said that we ought not to start home with less than one sack of flour and one of beans, even assuming we can get plenty of meat. Again he did not agree, glossed over all evident contingencies, and said something about its being only two days' rafting to Cook Inlet down Sushitna River, were the range once crossed. Hereabout it is impassible for horses, and returning, we should have to travel at least a hundred miles farther along its face, before reconnoitering for a pass in a region where all Government reports say there is probably no pass; cross the mountains, abandon the pack train, and raft. That would take two weeks at least—a sack of flour lasts one—but it is probably longer to raft down the Kuskokwim to Behring Sea. He heard me in silence, but I think my words told. I urged no return, and was all enthusiasm for exploring Peters. We agreed for that, anyhow.

And so we stumbled from a hedge of white granite bowlders to sparse spruces eating up along the roaring water, the first camp for a month in timber. There sat King and Miller, gazing at the sunset over the mountain, and a mighty tale they told of two big caribou killed, and a pair of hind quarters which was all one horse could carry.

Believe I've just eaten six steaks, and without salt, for it's nearly all used up, and we're saving a pinch to take up the mountain.

AUGUST 24.—Anyhow, I broke the record this morning by eating *nine* steaks, fat and rare. And walked it all off, chasing the horse four miles downstream.

While packing, Miller—thank Heaven!—was ordered to take Simon's place, going to camp up the glacier to-day; and no sooner that, but we made a discovery which sure must change our luck. Simon, glum at being left behind, plugged away at mending an old boot, instead of washing dishes—his duty. There's an awful itch in the fingers of our mechanical genius to tinker with something. Fred looked at him and said, "Whenever Simon tears his pants, he puts them away in his dunnage, and mends another pair, so as always to keep some play on hand." And if Fred sees him sewing, he calls out, "Whang-leather it!" Whang-leathers are the rawhide strips we use in place of twine.

But listen. When we crossed the glacier stream at last, to follow up its north bank to the ice, we saw chopped poles there arranged like a big clothes-horse, meaning an old camp. I investigated, first finding a pair of soggy overalls, and said "White men!" to Fred, because Siwashes would *never* discard a whole pair of overalls. Fred, swearing Indians had stopped there, said, "Don't Siwashes wear pants?" as I came on two mule shoes, and the Professor appeared with a camera film wrapper, saying, "Then your Siwashes have begun to take photographs." The while I spotted a red coffee can lying under a bush—opened it—white stuff was inside—looked like, felt like, tasted like—*was*—SALT! Last night Fred was pining to trade off our last fifty pounds of sugar "for one small five-pound bag of salt." Food is slimy without it. Fred wouldn't let the stuff out of his sight, and put enough for use on the mountain into his very dirty handkerchief, and hung it on his belt. The red canful we cached there.

Whose camp is this? What are white men doing here? Fred suggested that they are the "railway surveyors" that Brooks met last year headed hither from Tanana River. But I think the camp is this year's.[*]

Straight toward McKinley we headed, over the Peters moraine's endless hills. Soon, between its chaotic esker of irony bowlders, and white granite peaks, ponds the size of your hand glazed each valley, reflecting downward all the cloudy pomp of McKinley. Fed by silver threads from high, shriveled glaciers, they seeped down by hidden ways to the ice river. A caribou trail, for green moss edged the ice, led to the last alluvial fan at the great bend in the glacier, where you can throw a stone and hit the north wall of the mountain, pouring down glacier upon glacier under trailing cloud from 12,000 to 15,000 feet above the forgotten sea. Here we have camped (as an outraged old grizzly galumphed away, turning to think insulting

---

[*] An Alaskan Federal judge had been reconnoitering there.

things at us over his shoulder), but not on the flat by the stream, whence we could see up Peters, for the Professor pig-headedly insisted in pitching the tent close under the esker, away from water and view.

We climbed the moraine. "Yes, sir, yes, sir, sure as I live she leads over a low divide to Sushitna River," cried Fred excitedly of the mile-wide avenue of ice, the part heretofore hidden. It rose due south, cleaving McKinley from the front range, crumpling one huge arm against the main slope of the mountain, hanging countless stiff Niagaras on both walls. Yet no further than the middle of the long, sheer face of the mountain could we see, to which our line of vision is now parallel. There, under rose-colored precipices—the pink cliffs, we call them—the mountain plants a black haunch out into the sloping ice; nearer, the front range plants another. The glacier slips between them; vanishes. What is beyond? The Sushitna watershed? The headwall of this Peters glacier? The coveted south arête? What? As we wandered up there, altitude 5,000 feet, the Professor built a fire of moss—Fuegian moss, he calls it—just to prove it will burn. Of course it did, after these three clear days.

So we have eaten, cooking with the same old logs packed up to our first base. The Professor's tent is cocked high up on the esker. Here in ours, luxuriating in the space left by Simon, Fred says he can't sleep to-night for wondering what lies beyond the beyond of that next bend in the glacier. A strange man, he, indeed.

CHAPTER XV

KICKS, DISCOVERIES,
AND A DREAM

AUGUST 25.—Second Base Camp.

Late and lazily as usual we rose this morning and ate. The Professor, when all was skookum for a start onward up the glacier, exclaimed, "Oh, I haven't greased my boots yet!" So Fred and I dashed across the three bands of morainal chaos—colored black, then red, then gray, according to what rock the ice tears from the main wall in its resistless flow, and each band a mountain range in miniature—to the rotting névé in mid-glacier, strewn with white bowlders from the pasty granite front range. "Spick! Spick!" went the ice, yielding to hurried little surface rills cutting tortuous channels.

The plan was for all to ascend the glacier as far as we could, Fred and the Professor to remain overnight to see where horses could be taken, and explore for a ridge leading to the south arête of the peak. We carried light packs with two nights' grub for two, and the alcohol stove.

Soon dark cones rose truncated where crevasses had healed. We kept on fast. It was bully traveling. Slowly the imperious roadway all above snow-line unfolded, rose and extended with us; overpowered. Cones of a medial moraine forced us to its middle. We followed a thundering river through blue arch and tunnel of its own cutting. It squeezed us against the towering moraine, and deep in its bed we found a ford among big erratic bowlders.

The Professor and Miller appeared specks below in the distance, on the now white, crackly desert, which undulated like the oiled surface of a sea, where we trudged for hours, seeming not to move. Hanging glaciers, split by irony pinnacles, over-hung like Titanic crocodiles, gray-green and saffron, vomiting brown chaos into jagged black caverns, splitting smooth pillars of pearly marble, bearing ice beyond ice in dazzling levels and ample folds. Color? We had discovered color! The front range wall bore only atrophied ice, and far above us, over terraced lines carved in past years when the ice river was more Titanic, grew the Professor's darned, reddish Fuegian moss. An azure wrist—a snow-bridge—buttressed a huge detrital cone on the white plain, and beyond a city of brown pyramids huddled at the mysterious bend. One big feeder scruffed up under the "pink cliffs" in the cirrus gloom of three linear miles overhead, just tipped by the weak, slow-moving sun.

Fred waited for the others, dwindling like a flash into a speck. I kept on alone with beating heart. The ice swooped around the bend toward the front range, I with it. Was this a pass to the Sushitna? Fred had still been betting, "Give me four days' grub and I'll make Tyonek up this glaysher. Sure as I stand here, she goes down to the Sushitna. Easier than I thought. It's a cinch." You could not tell. Now the ice vanished around another bend, the dark buttress of the pink cliffs and into the mountain. Up there, I turned and looked downward.

The dizzy unworldliness of it all was intensified, compressed by perspective. You seemed suspended in air, infinitely near, yet infinitely far from ice or rock wall. The sky overhead was blue-black. The haze had dissolved, leaving rainbow islands of cloud at succeeding spheres of the shadowy cut, casting down abnormal shadows, swift darknesses, blazing revelations. Think of it—this mile-wide trail, unknown miles long, hemmed by one wall a mile high, another three sheer miles, and so straight you can hit its base with a snowball, as you look up at its summit, the apex of North America. Somewhere a snow-slide thunders, a tiny white cloud of fuzz like the puff from ten thousand cannon blurs the wall, its whisper dies away into the pre-creative silence.

I thought that the Professor might be sore at my tearing on alone, and discovering beyond the buttress; so I waited awhile in an ice cavern, invisible except to the rounded winter pallor of my pit, and the unreal sky. But I couldn't wait. Onward, I passed along the sheer black ridge cutting into the ice under the pink cliffs, heavy with four Alpine glaciers, and into the upper amphitheatre. The glacier bowed east. Suddenly a wall of ice peeked out from behind the buttress—ridged, pinnacled ice, growing into an enormous serac, the whole breadth of the glacier, massing into a white Niagara, hinting of the world's end, the unknown range, and the hid deserts of the moon. It towered, widened. I was planning to scale it and return before eating; but, aching with hunger, I saw the human trio behind crawling along an ice ridge, and waited. They caught up, and the Professor called me down—but only for the danger of glacier traveling alone. "If anything happened to you, it would be my responsibility," he said. Gosh!

We all ate zwieback and fried caribou chunks in silence. Then, at the great serac-foot, the Professor produced two horse-hair ropes, and insisted that we hitch together, by twos, Fred and me, he and Miller. We started up the ice-fall, struggling among its wrecked white skyscrapers that jutted out in cubes and blocks beyond gravity angles; crawled along little snow ridges, shinned miniature Matterhorns, where the sudden deeps were chill and ugly. A blizzard began. We tried lead after lead to the top of the chaos, but steepness and the driving snow herded us back.

It was four o'clock, and Miller and I should be starting, to reach the base camp where Simon was expected from the spruces. Each of

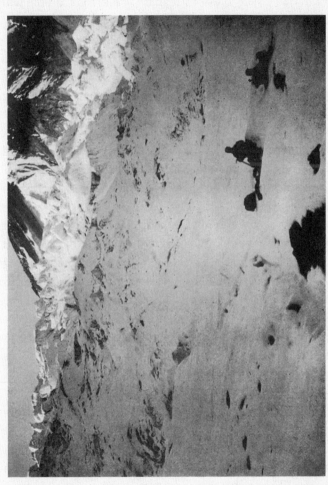

"The glacier bowed east. Ridged, pinnacled ice, massing into a white Niagara."

(Rounding the great west corner of Mt. McKinley.)

the others were carrying eight pounds, I fifteen. I delivered to Fred the hind quarter of caribou in my rucksack, enough to feed a family a week. He and the Professor would try to find room for the tent a little higher up. Suddenly the Professor turned, and in that storm where you couldn't see your hand before your face, said in his cocksure way that we should climb McKinley from the top of the serac; that he and Fred were going to stay up there for keeps. Having come up here on a reconnaissance, we had seen more bewildering glaciers and ridges than we could have imagined from below. "You other three can pack up the rest of the mountain outfit to-morrow, can't you?" added he. I said I thought that it was too heavy, but we'd try. Fred, as usual, said nothing. The Professor began naming over the stuff, forgetting all the heavy things. "You'll have Simon to help you," added he. Fred and I said that we didn't think that Simon could ever find the base camp from the spruces. "But we can't start up the mountain without him," objected the Professor. That capped my annoyance, and I reviewed my old protests about Simon, laying them a little thicker. "He's probably as opposed to your coming as you are to his," said the Professor. "Don't speak of us in the same breath," said I. "At least he's not such a kicker as you," said the Professor, and I retorted that it was generally self-respecting persons that kicked, for they know when they're being imposed upon. "This Jew'll stand anything you do to him," said I. "It's the Jew nature. And sometimes I can't help admiring him for it."

Scuttling back to camp, down, down, through the white skyscrapers, past the snowy pillars of Hercules, where the flakes thinned, by the hanging mound, and the polychrome moraine, to base camp on the flat talus in the rain—Miller said that I hadn't laid it on Simon heavy enough. The Professor stands more cursing of the kid from Miller than from me. And Miller isn't idle at it.

Going to bed just now, weary and burning in the rain, I said that the next expedition I was on would be my own. "For God's sake, count me in," said Miller.

Is Simon here? You bet he isn't. It's only eight miles straight up from the spruce, but bats are blind, and worms are deaf.

AUGUST 26.—Last night I had a horrible dream, such as comes in childhood, and usurps the next day's reality. It hung upon a name, and it's years since I've remembered dream-names. Miller and I slept together and all night as the drizzle peppered the tent, he regaled me with his Don Juan adventures in room ten of the Bohemia Hotel, Tacoma.

It seemed in the dream that I was very young, too. In all our kid games, I was made to go indoors long before dark, at first I didn't understand why, while other children still played outside. Growing curious at last, I would hide away down the lane back of the house at dusk, determined to see, or rather *feel* the mystery. Though I did so for days only, those days gave the vision a sort of cumulative horror, for years of mounting fear passed in that time; the sane experiences of advancing manhood, their heightened knowledge and pride in being, increased my sensitiveness to disease and shame of all unnaturalness. I came upon the creature near the barn. "The Nij, the Nij!" those words, his name, formed on my tongue. I saw him, a repulsive, deformed male, naked, pink, but very human, leaning upon one crutch appealing to me with some ghastly suffering. I burned with pity (and they tell me I'm hard-hearted). Slowly this waxed into a heart-sympathy, then into affection tempered with shame, for somehow I felt responsible for his living. He was a family dishonor, a skeleton from the closet of heredity, a breathing stain, which it wracked the hideous numbers of dream-fear to behold. He was the fruit of some loathly, indestructible family crime. Thus had I been guarded against him. It became a perverted passion with me to seek him out. I felt a blood-to-blood love for him, rooted in all his very unspeakableness and deformity. He would run away, but appear again, even follow me when I did not pursue. Once I cornered him in the shadows of the veranda of the house next door. I commanded him to speak, or I should beat his flesh. He began pleading with me for mercy, for relief from some agonizing thrall. My heart thrilled out to him. Tears in his eyes, he raised a long, shriveled arm, holding it pointed at me. The limb extended till it almost touched me—like the arms of changelings in Norse folk-lore—while he stood still. It was all but about my neck, the crutch too, growing longer and raised to strike, when—my mother walked down the veranda steps; and I woke.

Miller's stomach went on strike after we washed in the glacier stream. (It's half a mile from camp, thanks to the Professor, for the rock pool by the tent dries up every morning.) Miller had nausea and diarrhœa. Try as we could, the mountain outfit wasn't to be compressed into less than four forty-pound packs, and forty to the man is the limit for glacier work. No Simon, and we didn't expect him. Should I go up the ice with all I could carry? I thought about the Professor's order not to travel alone. But this was emergency, and by disobeying I might visit his fussiness upon him. Anyway, either Fred or he would have to come back for Simon, if climb he must. I decided to go; then not to; then chafed at lying still all day. I couldn't stay there. Miller saw me packing, and insisted on coming with me. We struggled over the colored moraine-mountains, I with all I could carry, he with lighter stuff—the kerosene cans. A thick drizzle set in, hiding your hand before your face. As we left, two sheep prowled on the great north wall near camp.

Miller stopped twice, exhausted, before we reached clear ice, where he caved in. I urged him forward to the lone cone of white rocks, where he cached his load tied in a rubber coat, and returned. Keeping on alone, I might as well have been blind in that fog. Under the weight I could take only six hundred paces at a time without resting; six hundred, six hundred, I counted each one, measuring out the eight miles. Now the long medial moraine, now the ice valley, now the lone cone held by the wrist of ice, where feeling left my shoulders. Now the blank glacier seemed a limbo, in which I must wander in circles, lost for ever; now the cloud-whirled vision of a feldspar paradise. It grew clearer. But never should I cross the plateau at the great bend, reach the huddled gravel cones!... Not till the long desert of the clear stream under the great serac, did Fred and the Professor appear as specks ahead. They looked from far, and stopped, seeing me alone; looked, and came on running. I met them where you walk on the face of a sheer wall to avoid the amphitheatre where I rested yesterday.

The Professor heard my story in silence. Fred, coming up, said, "What you bellyaching about?" and almost without being told, dashed on past down to camp, to find Simon. (Guess he was out of chewing tobacco, and you must always be tolerant with a chewer suffering so.) The Professor took less than half my load, and we climbed the serac, close to the main mountain wall, by a crafty combination of snow pinnacles, where I had urged going yesterday. For the first time we really had to rope among the black cliffs and rotting spires of ice and gravel. Then a snow slope steep enough to make us switchback, then another, and another. The tent specked the vast polar plain of the upper glacier opening suddenly before, seeming to retreat endlessly as we advanced....

Here, between the stern front range, and the southern haunch of the main mountain, a long, snowy spur makes out, reaching to the base of the steep rocks on its southwest shoulder—our old objective for the ascent, visible from Brooks' camp. The Professor says this new spur is to be our point of attack. We shall climb it, though the black rocks above still seem very steep.

Last night he and Fred had a hard time. Serac and storm forced them back, to ascend again as we have come. They camped in the dark; six inches of snow fell in the night, and an avalanche hurtled past a hundred yards away. To-day they went only a mile and a half beyond the tent, to the base of the snow spur, and saw little enough. They have explored almost not at all. A great reconnoissance, this! Yet the Professor has his dead sure route to the summit.

"We climbed the serac by a crafty combination of snow pinnacles."
(The great ice-fall of Peters Glacier.)

The glacier seems to turn on itself, east, around the snow spur, leaving a strange gap between the front range and the main mountain. Fred still persists that this leads over to the Sushitna, but we believe that it only faces Mount Foraker. The opening faces blankly into sky. Did they look through it? Oh, no; but they could have. Anyhow, I see the foolishness of an ascent by the front range, even could we have climbed it. We should have had to descend again thousands of feet, either into the gap by a long detour, or down here to the glacier. We seem on the right track now.

In the tent now the Professor's anticipations are working jubilantly. Alone with him, he's sometimes even companionable. But I wish his silent enthusiasm convinced. He's found *the* way up. It's positive, a certainty! We can't miss it. "Unless we have very bad luck." ("Ahem!" he rasps his throat), "I feel quite certain that we shall be on the summit of McKinley within five days." I hope so! Just now, over the pea soup, he has confided to me: "We shall spend a night on top. I don't think that that has ever been done on so high a mountain in such a latitude—why, I do not understand." So, another litter of his chickens is hatched out and counted.

I am really tired. Numbness from my arms has extended all over my body and deadened me. When I told the Professor, he said, "Your nerves are upset. I have noticed that lately." Rot!

He has just gone outside the tent to whirl the glass thermometer tube. The sun has set over the front range, and the cold orange and purple of night is flooding these enchanted white spaces. The frozen cataracts, ribbed upon the sheer desolation walling us, have yielded their flush to a waxen pallor of the crumbling, dusty hue of death. Between them gaps give down, whither you might likewise leap from a peak of the icy moon.

The snow packed about the edge of the tent is beginning to freeze. Soon we can touch the wall without a wetting. Well, my mackinaw is spread out on the tarpaulin, my poncho extending the tent-fly, and to serve as a pillow, too, with trousers and sweater on

The tent specked the vast polar plain of the upper glacier. ("Camp on Peters Glacier, altitude 7,500 feet, under the "pink cliffs.")

top. Now for caribou, cooked on the granite plate over the alcohol flame. Thermometer 22°, Altitude 7,550. Good-night.

AUGUST 27.—I thought that the Professor would never stir. We were awake for hours after daylight, but said nothing. I had nothing to say. The sun peeked over the pink cliffs about eleven, lit and melted the tent. "There, I was waiting for it," said he. Why so long, I didn't understand, unless he objects to mashing his feet into boots frozen like iron. But I was in no hurry, for yesterday's numbness still dulled brain, heart, and every muscle. We used up all our salt and alcohol frying caribou in the plate over the spirit lamp, and still hungry, leaving behind saltless meat chunks to eat at noon, divided the other stuff and hit out over the glacier snow broken yesterday, for the foot of the snow slope, two miles further up the ice. The tent, tarpaulin, and Simon's sleeping-bag, which the Professor has been packing, we spread out to dry.

On we popped our smoked glasses. The glare of this August sun is pitiless, though so far my eyes (which are very sensitive to light, so I had feared snow blindness) have stood it best of any. Swiftly our faces were burning and tanning at the same time to a Siwash copper color. The Professor complained of "lassitude," he called it, from the altitude and sudden cold. I felt like hell. We kept stopping to rest, spreading our mackinaws for a dry seat on the snow; then finding short cuts and safer courses around crevasses, poking hidden snow bridges with our axe handles. Glacier dangers don't worry me. I was drooling to the Professor, when suddenly I slipped to my waist down a fissure, and only paused to interject, "Oh, I'm down a crevasse."

We cached our loads, wrapped in a dry tarpaulin and weighted with a pemmican can, at the foot of the attack ridge. It is massive; rocky at the south end, but where we shall climb, steep and covered with enormous hanging bergschrunds.

We had toiled back to the tent by one o'clock, and ate the raw, saltless caribou. The Professor shied on his share, but up here I prefer raw meat to cooked, especially when half frozen. We burned with thirst, but couldn't get water till the Professor chopped a hole in a sealed crevasse, and stomached down, drinking till I thought he'd bust. Not once to-day did that sun melt a snowflake. I ate snow, against warnings of some terrible snow fever, which seems to be the Arctic explorer's bugbear. I have always eaten snow when I could, and don't see why being up on a mountain should stop me. Then I broke a tooth on zwieback, which reminds of Delphi's prophecy to Xerxes, when he broke his on the beach at Salamis. I've a conquest on, too.

No King, no Simon, no Miller appeared above the serac, as we'd expected, so down the great ice-fall we shinned again, the Professor discovering an alkali stream under the black cliffs. Clouds were boiling up the gorge. Onward, down, we trudged toward the base camp. At the amphitheatre, still no one; no figure specked the desert to the cones at the first turn, nor beyond. To forget the numbness in my feet and brain, I drew the Professor out about explorers' quarrels in the Arctic, pinning him to incidents when tempers flashed up; but he glossed them over, and excused all parties to them, mildly belittling their human meanings, till I could see where his prejudices lay, and understood why, lacking a ruling mind, he has become dull and gentle in self-defense—till at last, and the fourth time for me, we crossed that colored moraine range, and sighted the cotton tent in the drizzle. Not a soul in sight. We shouted. No answer. We opened the fly. There were King and Simon, sneakily sleeping in bags by a pot of cold pea soup. "What made *you* get cold feet?" said I to Fred, to revenge his challenge of yesterday.

They rubbed their eyes, and Simon told a pitiful tale. Unable to find horses in the lower camp, (didn't the Professor know he could never hunt a horse?) he'd started up here yesterday on foot. Halfway, hearing a whistle on the glacier—"just like the Professor-r-r-r's"—he had wandered out there, without seeing any one first, mind you; got lost, and spent the night on the ice. Only two hours ago Fred, having waited all day, sighted him from here, as he was hitting back for spruce, while in hail of camp. Deaf, blind, and stupid idiot! I kept my temper pretty well at this latest shine. He is sure a star explorer. Miller had hit down to timber with his coat collar turned up. The horses quit here days ago.

That whistling was a marmot, which toots just like a man, as any ass ought to have known.... And they have used up all the tea, except what's cached up on the mountain.

AUGUST 28.—The world's coming to an end, sure! The Professor got up first and started breakfast, the only time on the trip. Seems as if he's coming up to scratch, showing real head lately—he's so sure of success. We cut the heavy, useless buckles off our rucksacks and divided what's left of the mountain outfit into the three heavy packs, and for the fifth time I crossed the stony hell-rim, guiding the bunch in the dense fog and drizzle, by what is called "Dunn's air line," straight out to the lone cone where Miller's pack was cached. There we made four packs, forty pounds each at least, evenly as we could divide it.

Now, this was my third climbing of the glacier with a heavy pack, the first for the other three, for Fred and the Professor on that first day carried almost nothing. I called the Professor's attention to this, when he asked to have the stuff divided equally; but I made no kick, and took my good quarter of the load. Surely I haven't learned Fred's art of sitting around, offering to carry all the heaviest things, and ending up, after low soliloquies and foxy exchanges with the others' packs, having the lightest load. And Fred is always boasting that he can back-pack more than any two of us.

So again in single, silent file we toiled up that unearthly avenue. It's strange how spinal shivers from what has appalled weaken when you've seen the place once or twice; and how, after you suffer plunging into it alone, they are quite effaced in the artifice of companionship. The glacier was home-like to-day as some city streets I know. Absently I counted away all the landmarks, as the snow slides smoked and rumbled down the old pink cliffs.

At last, on top the serac, the human animal in each of us began to leer through the heroism of adventure. I guess that's always so. I was boiling peevish at Simon's squat, awkward presence. Each half a mile, we sat to rest silently on outspread ponchos on the new snow. Relative weights of packs were bruited once or twice, by Fred chiefly, but we forebore to argue, knowing that he had no chewing plug. Now he aggressively bet that his load was heavier than mine. Simon backed him, of course, so when we came to the tent, Fred folded it and tossed it to me saying, "Here, Dunn, I guess your pack's the lightest;" which I denied. So our mechanical genius rigged up scales with the tent-pole and an ice-axe. Dicker as they would, my load sank heavier on five tries. Fred kept on growling, till I said, "Lord, Lord we all admit you're the best back-packer. No one dreams of denying that." "Then I don't see how it is," began Simon, "that the lightest load always—" "You take a horse that hasn't done no work till he's fifteen years old," retorted Fred, "and of course he'll pack more than one's been worked hard all his life." The Professor only looked on and smiled. I admired him. Thus we climb McKinley.

At the cache under the spur, the gloom of the lunar-like night haunted the uncertain ice-field as we sorted the stuff, shiveringly guyed the tent with ice-axes, for tent pegs won't stick in the dry snow, and "tromped" (as Fred says) the névé on its petticoats, held down with the pemmican can, milk cans, and the two round red cheeses....

The tent is shaped like a herald's shield, so the Professor and I, being longest, are lying on the outside, fitting our bodies to the curve. He can't pump the Primus oil-stove aflame, and hands it over in disgust to Simon, who, as the owner of an auto in civilization, knows quite enough about vapors under pressure—thinks Fred, who hungrily swears at his fussy ways, *sotto voce*. The leaky tarpaulins and things are wadded under us, and the process of getting one by one into your bag, without wrecking the tent, is over; it's impossible when all are inside, so each is exiled in turn, out in the electric gloaming, putting on the Professor's mukluks, which he calls "finnsku"—the Greenland name.

The tea is coming to a boil. For water, we had to melt snow, as after a long hunt I could find no crevasse trickle. This uses much oil, and worries the Professor....: Simon is picking off the cover of the pot, and nervously putting it on again, which annoys Fred still more—"watched pots," you know,—and soon he will jab the milk can and pour all the milk into the tea, swabbing up with his finger what trickles down the side, eating it smacking his lips. Then he will save the can to drink out of, as it holds more than a cup....

We've had our first taste of pemmican, doled out by the Professor from his mussy corner, jabbed into chunks by Simon's knife. I'm for it. It's great; looks like mushroom spawn, and tastes like plum cake. It sure will stick to your insides.... Thermometer, 22. Altitude, 7,700 feet.

CHAPTER XVI

WHAT IS COURAGE?

AUGUST 29.—To-day we did not quite wait for the sun, and by ten o'clock were discarding the superfluities which your expert in "traveling light" always lugs to the very highest point to throw away. I left my binoculars (the Professor wanted me to quit my camera. Not I, as I think all his films are over-exposed) and the others abandoned enough wool underwear for a winter camp. "We need to concentrate on food, not clothing," announced the Professor, throwing away a sweater; and we started to break trail in the blazing, non-thawing sun, through eight inches of soft snow, toward the foot of this great spur or bergschrunds jutting from below the steep southwestern shoulder of McKinley.

The Professor says he is sure that its steepness must relax on its far, or eastern side, hidden from us by the spur. This seems plausible, and gives me hope, even considering how height and distance in this cold, dustless air, where 6,000 feet look like 60, and a door-step may be a half-mile cliff, knock imagination into a cocked hat. Of course we should have reconnoitered the slope, but how could we, with winter coming on, and our one sack of beans and one of flour five hundred miles from the coast? We have provisions for ten days, half of which was to be cached at to-night's camp, which was to be just below the steep place, at 10,000 feet, the Professor was certain; to serve as our base for the final attack and as a refuge in case we are driven back. Idle dreamer! You see, his programme is to reach the summit in about five days, returning in two or three.

The slope began easily, up the rough path of an old avalanche, but the packs were the sort that make you wonder how you can stagger on another ten minutes. We broke trail in turn; fifty paces each, then a rest, then, as we got used, seventy-five paces, and in an hour or so, a hundred. No one had spoken. Fred's "pass" to the Sushitna still gaped into blue sky, and the sheer 1,000 feet we'd risen above Peters seemed 200. Resting, we stamped a foot-hold in the névé, turned our backs skittishly to the slope, leaning against it on our packs; and once, doing so, came our first warning. Simon lost balance, and began to slip, slip, slip, as Fred caught him, and manœuvered him to safety, *i.e.*, saved his life. We all looked at each other and laughed, even Simon, all wiping the sweat from our burning faces with our arms; looked at our black-goggled eyes, which transform each fellow creature into a stranger; Fred a severe person, the Professor a funny big man, and Simon an aged clown.

Furtively, imperceptibly, the steepness had stolen a march on us. Névé ridges and humps of avalanche gave the only footing. As one line of foot-holds gave out, we had to sidle dexterously to another. In time the slides had scattered none at all. The steeper slope was swept clear and hard. Steps had to be cut.

Fred was ahead. He cut, cut, cut, with the cross-headed axe, slowly; laboriously balanced on one leg, trying the hole in the hard névé with the other foot; a new game for him, for us all; hole after hole, foot after foot. The slope braced upward into the bulging, overhanging walls of a huge bergschrund suspended over our abyss; higher, more of them hung, ending in two gigantic balconies, foreshortened against the sky. At last we could cut either to the right (southeast) toward the rocks which Fred had wanted to climb at the end of the spur (we've been going up its face), or to the left (northeast). We agreed, with no discussion, on the left.

We have only three ice-axes. Never giving them a thought this morning, all were gobbled up when we started, and I was left with the long willow tent-pole. It was never meant to balance you in half-cut steps that may or may not hold your toe, nor to clean out the granular stuff doused into one by Simon's laboriously lifted, stocking-stuffed hind leg. At the first shifts in cutting, no one wanted to trade an axe for the pole so I could cut. When at last I palmed it off on Simon, I wasn't too dexterous with the iron on the growing steepness. Soon they complained that I cut too far apart.

Yet we had risen. At last! A mountain looming through Fred's pass. "Foraker," said the Professor, though so small, distant, and snowless. It was two o'clock, the barometer only in the eight thousands, and it seemed you could spit into the tromped circle of last night's camp, and its black speck of superfluities. Some one said "Lunch," and when each had caught up, turned and staggered into his foot-shelf, I produced one of the red cheeses. The Professor cut it, and each mouth spit out its first bite—saltier than salt salmon, it is, here where water is worth its price in—oil. But each cached his piece in his red bandanna, and turned to pemmican, which pleased Fred, as the chunk in use is wrapped in a towel in his pack.

The Professor sighed—and led on. Now we cut steps in regular turn, the leader waiting after a hundred steps or so till the others had filed past, the man behind him cutting, as he fell to the rear, and so on, etc. Slowly we were forced to the sheer west edge, under the upper balconies. Should we try the narrow shelves that might run along its brow, or still zigzag up the steepening slope among the bergschrunds?—which last was chosen to be done, as nervelessly and carelessly as before. Fred settled it by saying, as he pointed to the right, "Hadn't we better take that swag?" as if we were driving horses on the tundra. He can't swallow, nor can I, these technical terms of alpining; a rucksack we call a backpack; serac, he daren't pronounce, it's "that steep place," and a bergschrund is "them over-hanging humps."

The swag started all right, then led straight up over the back of a big hump. The Professor led, cutting very slowly, shouting back how to avoid a hidden crevasse. Looking downward, the sheerness appeared poisonous to me, and I tried to think that I'd stick, in falling, on the fractional level just below, where loose masses of snow from the last slide from this very place still hung.

As the steps changed from a stairway to a step-ladder, the other three betrayed no excitement, no uneasiness. Neither did I at first, but I felt both; not dizziness, not vertigo, but simply the lightning, kaleidoscopic force of imagination, looking down the sheer two thousand feet, from where we clung by our toes, resistlessly told over how it would feel, how long it would last, what the climax in sensation would be, were I to fall. As hour succeeded hour, I lived each minute only to make the false step, cursing inwardly, but only at what then would be said by our civilized friends, their pitiful comments on this party, that with no alpine experience just butted blindly in to the highest mountain on the continent. Thought of that angered me. Cold feet, you say? Perhaps. But the personal test is yet to come. Courage is only a matter of self-control, anyway—and the tyranny of imagination....

Climbing McKinley with a tent-pole! Sometimes I boiled in those dizzy, anxious places that I had put myself in such a position with such men. My blind neglect of the Professor's silence on alpining now reproaches in another way. It's not bringing out his lack of staying power, as I thought, but his foolhardiness. Yet I must reap my own sowing. Once I asked if it wasn't customary to rope on such steep slopes, but no one but Fred answered, and he, "Y'ain't goin' to ketch me tied up to no one. A man don't want to take chances with any one but himself, haulin' him down from these places." And right he is....

One requisite of the explorer—besides aversion to soap and water—is insensitiveness. I understand now why their stories are so dry. They can't see, they can't feel; they couldn't do these stunts if they did. But the sensitive ones can't have their cake and eat it, too. They feel, but they can't *do*. As for me, is the doing of a thing to be no longer its end, as was in the old adventurous days? The telling of it the end instead? So I can't help admiring Simon and the Professor and their callousness, which is not bravery, not self-control. Their brains do not burn, horrifying the present with visions of the supreme moments of life. But it's better so. Where would we be, if there was another fool like me along? . . .

The Professor has been a real companion the last two days; intelligent and sympathetic. Probably he realizes that this is the final effort, and is making a grand play to come up to scratch. At any rate, to-night I'm convinced that he's really trying for all he's worth to get up McKinley; that this is the actual bluff I promised myself to make on the mountain. Even if we fail, the worst suffering will be over—the days following the first repulse—and then, Oh! how I shall feel for him, perhaps an undeserved pity, but it will turn all the tables of my regard. I shan't be able to help that. We are trying, damnably trying. . . . And all my righteous disgust and revulsion of race toward Simon have vanished. To-day we exchanged the brotherhood that civilized people do *not* fool themselves into believing is always the heroism of explorers in a tight place. I know it's hollow and meaningless; take away the danger, and all will be as before. But it's heroic while it lasts. And I've often felt I'd die for the semblance of such a thing in this life. . . . Forward and back, into the future and past, you can't see very clearly in these places. The brain works too fast, and your capacity to bear cold and hunger appals. . . .

I am morbid? Perhaps—but this is no place for cold sanity, for me, at least; though Fred and I on reaching this camp had a boxing-match—for warmth.

It was five o'clock and we were right under those balconies of the sky. One way led up, straight over the shoulder of a bergschrund, jutting like a gargoyle from a skyscraper. We climbed it; there seemed no lead further. The Professor said, "Camp anyhow, and we'll see."

We have camped, and on not ten square feet of primeval level. We've dug into the névé wall to get enough flatness to spike the tent, and contorted ourselves to place within again, I still on the windy side. And the wind is rising from the darkening white ridges and each unplanetary depth. The silk overhead shivers like cobweb, and jam down my head and cover up as I can in the soft snow, it steals through and stabs. Even in our warmth we're numb, tired, disappointed. We have come only half as high as the Professor hoped; we are only halfway to the top of the great snow spur, to the base of the doubtful rocks, to the camp for the final climb where the cache is to be made. So this brood of the Professor's chickens does hatch out dead.

"Tea or pea soup?" some one has just laughed. That will be the tag by which we will recall and laugh over this adventure. Simon has just remarked this. Thus, you see, self-consciousness is inseparable even from this sort of heroism. Perhaps after all it were best for us to slide off this gargoyle quietly as we sleep—as it keeps haunting me we shall—or better, that this ugly white beak shall fall with us senselessly in the night. I have just touched on the possibility of this, aloud, and Simon remonstrated, adding, "We don't want to speak of such things, even if we feel them!" What sickening insincerity, as if that could make the snow any firmer!—to choke the dizzy sense of danger, which is the very thing that's brought us here—as if in this quivering suspension over the vast polar world, it were not criminal to be acting a part....

Fred watches Simon fussing with the stove, much annoyed. The Professor is scribbling in his notebook—inches, feet, and degrees I suppose. How warmly the tea went down!—with dirty chunks of the crumbled zwieback, which the Professor draws from a white bag and throws at us with a "Here's your ration, Dunn." Two cups each; first you dip it out of the pot, then when it's low enough, you pour, spilling it on the sleeping-bags. Fred has corralled the empty milk can from Simon. We can't afford to melt snow for a "squeeze." Then the pemmican—all you want. It's scraping the roof of my mouth sore. Simon is telling how to run an auto. We are all laughing now. This is all a great joke; there's something very devilish about just being here. Every one is in a bully humor, more tolerant of his fellows than ever before on the whole trip. For aren't we the only ones in all this dastardly white world? How would it pay for the only four creatures in the universe to be the least at odds? We depend on one another. And yet, perhaps our devotion is—only the warm tea....

I have been outside, forgetting to undo the safety pin that holds the flap, and nearly tearing down the tent—as Fred almost just did. The finnsku do not give a sanded footing, and you slip around on the inches of the gargoyle, expecting to be floating down through mid-air, your stomach feeling inside out.... Not an acre of the forbidden tundra was to be seen. Through Fred's gap, which leads even west of Foraker, and circling the dead, whitish granite of the front range and its three crocodilian glaciers, sleeps a billowy floor of summer cloud, into which the sun is blazing a vermilion trail, lighting the gentle Siwashes of Bristol Bay far west, perhaps, or a slow-smoking island off the coast of Asia. That vast, glimmering floor of cloud! At last, the silvery lining for us of what may be gloom to all the world, an enchanted plane cutting the universe, soft and feathery, yet strong and bright like opal—for us and us alone; veined and rippled, dyed with threads of purple, rose, and blue, where Foraker rises pale with late sunlight, like the ramparts of a new-created heaven, blushing a moment for us alone....

I can feel the death-like silence. No one is asleep, yet no one dares move, lest he tell his neighbor he's awake. A cold blue from the nether world forms with the awful twilight a sort of ring about the tent, which magnifies the texture of the silk, and rises and falls as I lift my head from its pillow of trousers and pack. It is a sort of corrupted rainbow, or what the halo of a fallen angel might be like, I think—the colors burned and wearied out. The world below is swinging on through space quite independently of us, at least. I am not cold, but I shiver, and shiver; think and think of everything I have thought and feared to-day, and the little of it put down here. And if I doze I seem to be at the very instant of slipping off the gargoyle in the finnsku....

We hang our snow-glasses on the tent-pole, knotting the strings around it, so they dangle down. They look very funny up there, motionless above me—four of them, mine the lowest.

CHAPTER XVII

PUTTING YOUR HOUSE
IN ORDER

AUGUST 30.—Not a word as we crawled from the tent toward nine this morning, and draped the gargoyle with tarpaulins wet from underneath, and sleeping-bags wet from feet and breath. Fred and I were awake, as usual, from a small hour, shooting anxious glances at the Professor, knowing it was no use to rouse his sigh— till I remarked aloud that the sun wouldn't reach our shelf till four P.M., so he turned over, threw us our pemmican, Simon lit the stove, and we told our dreams.

Just an "I suppose" from Fred, starting ahead, settled our direction, straight up, a bit to the right (S.E.)—Oh, yes, steeper than anything yesterday—houses are not built with such sheer walls as that slope began with, only began. Packs were the same, numb shoulders ached the same under weight of the deadly cheeses, for what use was a depot on that snow clothes-peg? We crawled along a crack in the névé, where you had to punch holes for your frozen hands to hold you there in the crumbly stuff, and looked down a clear 3,000 feet.

Whew! Those next four hours! I had the tent-pole, of course—no one would touch it on this stretch. All yesterday's torture in fears, regrets, from this life-blighting imagination reassailed me on the quivering brink of the END. We stopped, staggered with set faces, crawling around each step-cutter to let him gain the rear; so slowly leaned back to rest, carefully fitting heels into toe-nicks, backing upright against our ponchos; but more often rested with face to the slope, bowing down heads flat over the abyss, to let the packs bear straight down and ease shoulders, so the nether white glare swam upside down between your legs.... A hundred times I concluded (and am still convinced) that I was not meant to climb mountains; a hundred times more I called myself a fool, seeing the awkward rears of Simon and the Professor; clutching the tent-pole, again and again I turned just for the delicious suffering of seeing the hateful Below spring upward, as in desperation you pound a hurt to kill yourself with pain—to make the worst seem WORSE, knowing that THIS is not the moment when I must slip, but this, the NEXT, MUST BE; with Foraker leaping like a rocket into the sky, the far, pond-spattered tundra sweeping skyward in waves, a sort of dullness before the snow chokes off ALL....

And yet time passed like lightning. I could not believe the man who said that it was 2:20 P.M. The Professor was in the lead. It was my turn to cut, but he did not seem inclined to take the tent-pole and give me the axe. I offered and offered the pole, but couldn't tell if he withheld the axe because he thought I'd rather stay behind, or didn't want to give it up. I was content enough behind, but I felt he thought that he was sort of sacrificing himself to me. "It's all ice here. Look out," he would say calmly between most deliberate steps, and stopping to hack a little deeper. "Are they too far apart?"—just the things I should say ahead there, *but I was not saying them;* that made me feel guilty; words of big consolation; I admired him mightily. Fred and Simon never spoke, except at rests, and then horrible little commonplaces.

"We could dig a seat now, on the corniced brow of Fred's rock ridge."
(Resting at 10,000 feet on Mt. McKinley.)

Everything was ice, not an inch of névé. It seemed to take ten minutes to cut each step, which then held one toe, or one inch of a mushy, in-trod boot-sole. Nothing for mittened hands to grip. I asked Fred what he thought of climbing with the tent-pole. "Yer couldn't make me use it on these ice places," he said. And Simon—think of it—said, "The man with the tent-pole oughtn't to have to cut steps at all." But we kept on as before. "It's getting a little leveler," said the Professor. It was. And then I would ply him with questions about that leveling, laughingly fishing for more assurances. "Rocks ahead, the edge of a ridge, something, see them," he said. So there were. "Thank you, thank you," I said, as if that were all the Professor's doing. "God! I admire the way you take this slope," I'd exclaim. And by heaven, with all these mean pages behind, I still do.

We could dig a seat now, on the corniced brow of Fred's rock ridge, 1,000 feet sheer down, then down 1,500 of black, porcupine-like spires. Lunch? No, no one was hungry. As usual we asked for the barometer. As usual, the Professor said, "It can't have responded yet," drawing it from his belt. It was not quite 10,000 feet.

I led at last with Simon's axe, straight up toward the objective rock slope (N.W.). We were above the balconies over last night's camp. Soon the snow softened to let you step sometimes without cutting, then again all was steep as ever. On the east, a huge ridge paralleled ours, depressed in the middle with a squarish gap, through which a dark, greenish line wavered in the sunlit haze— low peaks of the Sushitna valley flecking the horizon. So we could see on the great range's other side. Then toward Foraker, through that gap, gathering all the southern ridges about the final bend in Peters, and yet beyond all, rose and rose a turret-like summit, smooth, white, specked with huge bergschrunds, to a terrifying height. "There's a high mountain* over there," I shouted, "just appearing. You can't see it yet. A new one!" "Yes, sir, yes," said Fred, catching up, and we sat down to gaze and gnaw pemmican.

In half an hour we stood here on the narrow knife of the spur-top, facing failure. Ahead, the zenith suddenly petrified into a big, pinkish-yellow strip of rock, offending the sight as a thunder-clap might have deafened. The Professor dropped his pack and ran on, mumbling an order to camp at the first flat spot, dashing through the deep snow toward our coveted ridge, now so black and puny. I saw it was hopeless.

The yellow strip shot downward, between ours and the Sushitna ridge; down, down, like a studded bronze door, straight into the reversed head of Peters—three thousand feet down, three thousand feet above; a double door, for a straight gorge cut it in twain, a split not glacier-made, but as if this apex of the continent were cracked

* Mt. Hunter, about 15,000 feet.

like an old plate. Slides roared, the whole swam in snow-mist, and two turret-like summits far and high to the east, grew gold in the late light.

Here, where the black ridge leading to the top of the pink cliffs should have flattened, all was absolutely sheer, and a hanging glacier, bearded and dripping with bergschrunds, filled the angle between.... To-morrow? Here in the tent, not a word has been said. I wonder, has any one admitted to himself that we're checkmated, or would, if he realized it? How sure is the Professor of spending a night on the summit? Looks like another brood of dead chickens....

The old cooking, squirming, changing-sock game is on. I am digging névé to melt—"finest imported névé," we laughingly call it—from a snow hole at my head, where the kerosene has not spilt to flavor it. Fred glum. Simon at the stove. The barometer has adjusted itself, but only to 10,800 feet....

The Professor has just come in from a long meditation outside. "Never, never," he says, "have I seen anything so beautiful." That from him! The Spirit of the North, like Moses, has struck water from the rock. But it's so. I've seen it. No cloud-floor hides the forbidden tundra, no mist softens the skeleton angles of these polar alps; only a wan red haze confuses the deeps of the universe, warning that they, and we, and life at last, is of another world. The tundra dazes; its million lakes, lifted by refraction mid-high on the front range, are shapeless, liquid disks ablaze; and the crazy curves of their shores far below, which may be the dark and sleepless land—no eagle could tell—are walled by pillars of smoky violet, verily from against the sea....

Last night I tried to hide my fear with sophistry. Now to be honest. I dread the descent more than the climb. I believe that there's too much ahead in living to have it all cut suddenly off against your will in a fool business; and if it must be, there's no use shivering about it. If I had any beliefs, I'd put my house in order. Where this sort of thing leads a man, God only knows. Anyhow, we're not on a

"The zenith suddenly petrified into a big, pinkish-yellow strip of rock, offending the sight as a thunder-clap might have deafened ... I saw it was hopeless." (From our highest camp on Mt. McKinley. The wall that checked us.)

shelf that may break off. Good night. Pleasant dreams, and hear me whine in my sleep to the Professor—if I sleep.

AUGUST 31.—Alone in the tent. It's about noon, and the sun is blinding over the yellow wall. No one stirred till late. After breakfast, orders were given not to pack up. Fred and the Professor walked toward the cliffs.... I can see them now, sitting on a cornice where the ridge narrows. They are no longer staring at the yellow wall.

Simon and I have been talking. This is how I did put my house in order: "Simon," I said, "I want to apologize to you for everything unkind or offensive that I've done or said to you on this whole trip." He laughed, looked away, and said, "Oh, that's all right." Tears came to my eyes. Then I felt ashamed, then angry. Then we talked as if we'd been brought up together; he of dangers of ships in the polar sea, I of old days in Alaska. I said that I was certain we could get no further. He changed the subject.

Fred and the Professor have just returned. Neither spoke till right near the tent, and looks lie through snow-glasses. "Make tea, and put a whole can of milk into it," said the Professor. While taking in the bags and tarpaulins from the sun, I heard Fred say, "It ain't that we can't find a way that's possible, takin' chances. There ain't *no* way.... We thought it might be managed on that hangin' glacier first." Simon burst out in surprise. "Professor-r-r, you're not going to give it up, are you?" and began pointing to ridges and glaciers right and left, saying that of course we must go down and then up by them. The Professor tried to reason with him. Simon seemed straining points, but I was shamefacedly admiring his determination, when Fred came into the tent, and said, "A holler like that makes me sick." Is it a holler? I guess it is, which makes me feel smaller than ever. It doesn't matter. We're going to start down.... Something besides courage and determination is needed to climb a mountain like this. Forgive me, if I call it intelligence....

Simon pretended that he wanted to lug down the twenty-pound tin of pemmican, but we kicked it off the ridge, and started descending on the run. How I got over the ice above Fred's rocks, don't ask. I've heard of persons sweating blood, and red stuff kept dripping from my forehead, as step by step, face outward into the dancing gulf, we tottered over the ice ladder of two days' cutting. I talked incessantly to the Professor of the various sorts of courage; how easy it had been for me to stand on the crater-edge of Mount Pelee, just after St. Pierre had been destroyed, because life or death there *was not in my own hands,* as here; and so new problems bothered me about cowardice and responsibility, which I've not solved yet. Half way down, the Professor insisted on my taking his axe for the tent-pole, for which I put him forever on Olympus, between Leonidas and Brutus. Thus at last we strung along Peters, each stopping dazedly in his tracks now and then to gaze back and upward. Now at the Professor's and my lone camp of the week ago, we are in our eiderdown, on the ice just above the serac, in the messy disorder that it seems we've been living in forever.

CHAPTER XVIII

RAVENS AND DOOMED HORSES

SEPTEMBER 1.—To-day, as I geologized alone on the glacier, the others dashed below to the spruce camp and Miller. I did not reach it till dark.

That endless, lone walk, past the lower reaches of gravel and chaos, out again upon the flat, forbidden tundra! Generations had passed since it had oppressed, warned, inspired, and all to no purpose. It was just the same, as must be the world to a criminal after trial and false acquittal. Ravens circled overhead, following confidently. "You're caught, you'll die," they seemed to jeer. "Can't get out of this country before winter. You're fools, but we like human carrion. We've got you. Ha!" And aren't they right to be so hungry and hopeful about us, with our one remaining sack of flour, one of beans, and civilization, as we have come from the Pacific, forty-eight days' distant? All the meat has rotted. All the horses are lost, having slipped our dear clothes-mending Simon before he joined us on the mountain. Miller, hunting a week, has not found them.

I came upon the four sitting in dead silence about a dying camp-fire in the weird but friendly timber. They had only just reached camp, having found the Brown Mare far up along the ice, with a snagged foot, and so useless to us any more, and helped her in. "I never thought you fellers would be back so soon," said Miller in his low voice, taking me aside. It sounded like an accusation of cowardice. In his heart of hearts, I know he thinks us quitters; but that's human nature, for he was ambitious and wasn't with us. No use ever to explain.

Now I can think better about yesterday. We were checkmated by steepness at 11,300 feet (by the Professor's aneroid) with eight days' mountain food on our hands. But remember this: also with scarce two weeks' provisions below on which to reach the coast, and winter coming. The foolishness of the situation, and the fascination, lies in the fact that except in this fair weather, unknown in Alaska at this season, we might have perished either night in those two exposed camps. Even the light wind nearly collapsed the tent, and any alpinist will tell you what storm and six inches of snow on that sheer slope would have meant. But where fools precede angels, the drunkard's providence goes along, too. I don't think the slope we did climb would have worried an experienced mountaineer, who might succeed on the yellow wall above. I should like to see one there—but not a Swiss or a Dago.

SEPTEMBER 2.—Again life is a horse-hunt.

Down the river for miles are only old tracks in the sparse spruces; on the back trail, no lead across the crick five miles away. Hunting alone, I have the dear, Munchausen-like dreams roused by the wild tundra when the buck-brush is scarlet, cranberries are ripe, and winter's in the North. Hunting with Fred and Miller (after losing Simon) I hear the few last chapters in their life-stories, which give the final key to the real manhood of these two. To-day as we lazed on the hunt, eating blueberries, Fred told of the girl he had been in love with when first he went to Montana in '83; how he started to travel east to Iowa in prairie wagons with her and her parents, paying his way by chopping wood for them. But he never married. He hid his sentiment with funny tales of buckskin-clad female rounders met on the way. Miller told how after capsizing in a small boat off Vancouver Island, he went home to his mother who had heard that he was drowned. And, as we ate the sour, fermented berries, we gazed into the aching dimness of the tundra, and wondered if that stream bed, scarcely outlined so far away, turned to right or left toward the Yukon, behind that gnomish range of hills. And all through these endless, vain hours, those eager ravens with their silken death-rustle swooped overhead.

Late this afternoon, Simon and Fred came in with the two Grays, Big Buck, P.R., and Whiteface. We saddled them, and till twilight would catch sight of one another, gliding into reality, vanishing, on distant swells of the tundra, like horse-and-rider statues. The Professor, on a Gray, crossed the stream to hunt, knowing no beast would have wandered there. And we found no more....

Miller and I to-night had just finished eating a mess of cranberries stewed in moose-grease and condensed milk, when in comes Simon, and we give him a taste. It so tickles his palate, he dashes off to make a mess of it for himself, blindly picking the handiest red berry—the poison, bitter kind that grows on a bush. He almost swore, and shaving by the fire light I cut myself from laughing. I had been watching a bully, big, gray wolf haunt the opposite river bank, for we've thrown the spoiled meat right under the bank near camp. I lay flat in the brush and studied his big bushy tail, lithe as a cat's. He vanished for a long time. Suddenly, right at my head, I heard a great rattle of stones, but when I jumped up, Mr. Wolf and a hind quarter of the meat were gone.

We've been discussing how to get out of the country, for ice is beginning to rim the river slews at night. Twelve days' rafting down the Peters stream should bring us to Tanana river and a Yukon trading post. But northeast stretches mile on mile, white with 10,000-foot alps, and the flat avenues of the world's biggest inland glaciers, ramifying like the tentacles of a cuttle-fish this supreme American range. And it is all unmapped, undiscovered, bleak and shriveled under the breath of autumn. And south across these mountains, to the Sushitna River and Cook Inlet, the Government Survey report we read between chapters of our one and only Tom Sawyer, says with familiar triteness that it is "extremely doubtful" if any pass exists.

That challenged us. That settled it. We will find that pass, and most of us for a separate reason. We were all wonderfully in accord, deciding without argument. Miller, Fred, and I would take all risks crossing the mountains, for the very sake of them, and the unutterable rewards of discovery; the Professor agreed, because finally defeated on McKinley he thought, (so he said), he must propitiate science by some sure-enough exploration. And Simon declared that he wanted to reach the Sushitna thus in order to attack the south side of McKinley—on the two teaspoonfuls of tea we have left, blizzards, and zero weather. His "hollers" are still in order, and our flashes of heroism on the sheer névé have burned out and left us frail with the human passions of again hitting the long, long trail behind a pack train—which is more the test of manhood, I hold (if you do any work), than cutting steps on the perpendicular.

Miller bets we'll be only two days going to rafting water on the Sushitna. I took him.

SEPTEMBER 3.—All horse-hunting but the Professor, who lazed in camp.

Fred and I late this afternoon struck a tributary of the Peters stream far below where any of us had gone before, and there came upon the freshest horse tracks yet. We counciled, as in war. We couldn't trail the beasts and get back to-night. We had seven horses already, enough to cross the mountains with. We are eating into the last sack of flour, and still out of meat, having no time to hunt, though to-day this pondy country all about the horizon was alive with caribou. We decided to return to camp, and argue on these grounds with the Professor, for a start to find a pass to-morrow. We did.

Back there, he heard us, and agreed, ordering all extras to be thrown away. But I notice that the Professor is keeping all his junk, and Simon is holding on to his stray overall patches, bits of leather, tooth-brush, and the glass thing he snuffs catarrh cure into his nose from. At supper Miller and I found his college flag, which he boasted in New York he was going to wave from the top of McKinley, and we—wiped the dishes with it.

So seven horses remain to die. Perhaps that ought to worry us, but it doesn't. They will have a better chance to pull through the winter here, rustling grass through the light snow of the interior, than on the Sushitna side of the range, where it is very heavy, and we shall abandon the others. Also much depends on their physical condition, which should be good now; they should have fattened while we were on the mountain. Ought we to find and shoot them? I for one could not stand by and see horses that have served and suffered for us dumbly, on such a grind in such a land, shot in warm blood. It would be too much like murder; better to kill some humans. And I hold this allowable human selfishness. We measure others' suffering in terms of our own pain, and if we're far away at the momentary wrench when others die, effectively no suffering exists. At least this cowardice is the custom, and such sophistry the perquisite of Alaskans, though in civilization you will condemn it. No prospector will ever shoot his horse.

SEPTEMBER 4.—This evening we packed, and were off. Our route lies northeast, along the north face of this great east-curving range. Ahead, we can see that it throws spurs and ranges out into the tundra, but we shall keep as near to its heart as possible, right at the moraine heads of its glaciers.

From here our course leaves Brooks', who struck out among the hills on the tundra, reaching the north-flowing Cantwell River, thence the Tanana and the Yukon. The head of the Cantwell breaks far into the range, and has been used as a pass traveling north from the Sushitna, but we hope to find our pass south, in an opposite direction, a hundred miles this side of it.

We halted at a large flat of tangled streams to hunt caribou; Fred stalking toward the mountains, Simon tiptoeing close behind, like a comic dwarf. Shots crackled under a morainal hill, and the Professor, thinking them misses, bungled the train across a willow swamp, where we floundered waist-deep. But under the hill, there were Fred and Simon standing by a big dead moose, with sixty-four-inch horns. They had executed a clever sneak, and shot him from a few yards, as he looked the other way, quite unawares. "The old cuss was sort o' logy," said Fred, "jes' ready to git off an' rut." The Professor insisted on propping up his head with sticks, and photographing him as if he were a bull lying alive in a pasture. "Now take him with his slayer," said the Professor, and Simon, who hadn't fired a shot, dashed in and posed by Fred.

But five sacks of meat and sixty pounds of tallow he has given us, and the kid has cut off his dewlap for a cap.

SEPTEMBER 5.—A goshawful horse-hunt. Season, failure, being homeward bound—nothing changes *that* torture.

Simon and the Professor lazing about camp, Miller, Fred, and I started to back trail for the beasts. Simon's excuse for loafing is that he has to wash the dishes; but though we're gone hunting for hours, he seldom has it done when we get back, and then begins packing the things as you put rings into a jewel case, but so most of them get squashed. Fred and I can never find what we want to cook with at night.... Toward noon I saw the beasts on top of a mountain, just sneaking down the other side. They had been in full sight of the camp for an hour, so the Professor said afterward. I had nearly busted my heart making the 3,000-foot ascent for them, and met Fred on the summit. And at camp they had seen us and the beasts before we saw them, and never shouted, or started after them! "Oh, we thought you'd see them before long," said the Professor. Da— Christopher!

Toward afternoon we approached the flat, gravel desert of Muldrow glacier, named by Brooks, and the largest on the north face of the range. Far beyond it, out upon the tundra, smoke rose from a squat hill, the first human sign for two months. Indians? White men who have found our lost horses? We lit the moss in vain answer to that heartsick expanse, where far away glittered Lake Minchumina, near where Herron all but starved four years ago, a streak of silver through the haze. So we have camped at the far end of the great willow flat under the frozen brown estuary, which is four miles broad if a single inch; and three miles from water.

Reaching camp every night now, I say aloud:

> There was a man in our town,
> And he was wondrous wise.
> He jumped into a bramble bush,
> And scratched out both his eyes.
> But when he saw his eyes were out,
> With all his might and main,
> He jumped into another bush,
> And scratched them in again.

Simon laughs and repeats it; but he doesn't see the point: that McKinley is the Professor's first bramble bush, and the pass is to be the other—I hope.

Miller and I are "trying out" moose-fat in the pots. You cut it up into small squares, fill pans full over the fire, and pour out the melted grease to harden in old baking-powder tins. The gut fat is best, and makes bully "crackles" for eating. At last, Fred admits what I have always insisted, that caribou is better eating than moose—probably because we have no caribou now. Every mouthful we eat swims in grease. We use it for gravy on the beans. Goodnight. Overhead rise the miniature hills of the moraine, icy in their depths, but yellow with dying cottonwoods.

SEPTEMBER 5.—It's all an undiscovered country, virgin to white men's eyes—this bare, cold moss, these cloudy glaciers. And yet—

> "I have been here before,
> But when or how I cannot tell;
> I know that keen, sweet smell—"

That's wrong, but how *does* it go, and what is it from? ... I've done too much discovering. I'm unimpressed, jaded.

We veered a bit east to-day, following up the north side of the petrified Muldrow desert, into the great space north of McKinley and the Sushitna head waters, which is blank on all maps. The horses had wandered three miles back to the Muldrow stream, and Fred and I, chasing them, saw two big black animals lurching through the willows of the flat. "B'ars, by gum," said he, "else very dark moose. They move too slow for caribou." Packing up, no one could find Fred's ice axe. (We still keep the axes, why, I don't know, unless for souvenirs.) We tore up the ground hunting it; every one thought it had vanished through the other's carelessness, and no one believed his fellow's protest and innocent tale. Evidence was that Simon had used the axe to dig a water hole last night—when lo! Fred found it himself, under a willow bush. Starting, we followed a stream parallel to the ice, where the Professor traveled so slowly, the horses jammed behind a bowlder hanging over the torrent. One by one, they took to the water and swam across. We tried in vain to stone them back, till the Professor, seeing whose fault it was, made a grand-stand dash, and coralled all on our bank again. He was sore with us, and showed it by hiding it so well.

Noon, and we struck down into a broad silt plain heading into large glaciers from the range's heart behind Muldrow, and ate our boiled moose bones. We mounted a low, grassy saddle, and entered a broad valley opening before, which cut at right angles, against all reason, through the bounding peaks of the range. We traveled between pale, clinkery walls. The valley was two miles broad; we kept along its southern wall, and toward four o'clock a mountain jutted into its middle.

Making camp, we climbed it. Far away southeast, McKinley rose like an unearthly castle of opalescent glass, wrapped in the streaked, cold clouds of a Turner sunset; its summit, now seen from a different angle, a wilderness of peaks and gullies. We stared at it, seeing no better route up those steeps; looked wonderingly, and no longer in guilty silence. Northeast, the valley still keeps on far as the eye can reach, and far ahead, where a stream cutting it at right angles broke through the northern wall to the tundra, we saw spruces—think of that, for we've almost forgot how trees look!—stealing upward and dying away on its bleak, flat opens. Fred even refused to believe his eyes saw timber.

The Professor has just "worked out our position," with a map, a pencil, and a straw. Now he travels with his wooden compass in his pocket, the Abney level tied on the Light Gray (the new lead horse—for L.C. is one of the lost), poor beast, loaded to the ground with the junk boxes. We've lugged pounds of instruments which haven't been used at all, and now we're lugging them home. Noble apology for adventuring, this science! "There's a good chance to use your theodolite now," said Miller to-day, pointing to an angle of Muldrow, whose direction of flow we'd been arguing about. The Professor only smiled, and never touched an instrument—as often before when we've wanted an observation. Sometimes as we plug along I feel, from what I've seen here and elsewhere, that not much will be done in Northern exploration till it gets into the hands of some one Napoleonic, brutal, perhaps, but with a compelling *ego* and imagination; away from the bourgeois and cranks.

We're camped in a steep gully on the valley's right. Miller and I have been digging out chunks of lignite from the stream to cook to-morrow's breakfast with. Now for bed, and the school-room scene from "Tom Sawyer," before dark. Every one corrals horse blankets, and sleeps on a dais of them these icy nights. But we don't smell moldy any more. Good-night!

SEPTEMBER 6.—On through our broad valley, U-shaped, and therefore glacier-carved, we still veer east with the eastward trend of the great range. Slate, which hints of the Sushitna watershed, re-placed the porous pink porphyry to-day, and we nooned by beds of lignite bursting out of the ground like big truffles. On the flat of the wooded stream seen yesterday, but far above where timber had pe-tered out, lay—a crumpled piece of birchbark. Bark cut by a knife! held by human hands!—and no birch grows on this side of the mountains!

It must have been carried from the Sushitna valley; but Siwashes or white men here? Never! Our valley cuts all streams at right angles on their way north to the Yukon, and we cross just under their gla-ciers, while the mountains are thickening ahead. So I was hot to ex-plore for a pass up this stream's valley, though I believe that we can cross the range by almost any of these ice rivers, 'spite of the Gov-ernment. But no; the Professor would listen to no hint, and looking toward the ice, sighed, "It's following the line of least resistance to keep on." Line of least resistance! Hell! and Fred was mad, too.

So we dragged up the poor beasts again from the flat to the valley level; and camp is by a salt lick, a giant clay sore breaking through the tundra, where the beasts are swabbing their tongues in its cold mud....

First cut in rations to-day. We're limited to two biscuits each at breakfast. Its panful must last for lunch, and at night we must ask the Professor's permission to cook more. He's taking notice with a vengeance about grub and cooking. He used to expect us to bring him food like genii. Now he loves to chop green willows and insists on smothering the cook fire with them. They do give a hotter blaze, but if we always waited till they flamed up, we'd never get to food and bed.

Now the Professor is ascending a clinker hill with the wooden compass. Far ahead, queer slaty peaks, crimped and steepled, seem to choke the valley. We've followed it for thirty miles.... Ice is forming around the willows of our stream.

SEPTEMBER 7.—To-day, two low ridges ribbed the valley transversely; two more large glacier streams cut it, draining 10,000-foot peaks at the heart of the range, which stared at us crookedly for hours. We traveled eight miles, swinging to N. 72° E., and killed a fat caribou with thirty-five-point horns.

Since all valleys seemed equally good for a pass, and all were condemned, I thought that we should keep on through the low black spurs ahead, which must drain into Cantwell River, as it eats far into the range, causing what we geologists call "stream capture." I supposed that we were now bound for the Cantwell's known pass to the Sushitna. Again no; we struggled up that first conglomerate hill blocking the valley, and having chewed our cold boiled caribou, hit the stream beyond. We followed it up. Beyond the higher hill ahead, the country was rougher, but not impassable, and the main range was plainly lower there, promising a pass wherever you wanted. But the Professor ordered camp on the sparse willow flat, two miles below the stream's ice. We halted. He ran out across the flat to look at the glacier, hid by a crook of rock. I followed. Nunataks rose like carbon needles from the cloud-hung fields. Its gorge seemed less promising than any condemned; yet—"We'll

find a pass up here," ordered the Professor. "There was a man—"
muttered I with fervor.

Not a blade of grass grows here, and all the pea-vine is dead. It's
wonderful how spry the horses keep on almost no feed at all.
"Pretty poor pickin', but it's the same everywheres," says Fred.
Every minute or so the beasts start hot-footing on the back trail,
and one of us—never Simon—scoots after them on the run.
Ptarmigan are flocking in bands of hundreds in the bare willows.
Now we are watching Simon chase sheep on a near mountain, the
animated snowballs stringing out in a flying wedge as they see him
rise like a rock mannikin above. The winter sunlight lies on dark
peaks, growing ever mightier as they fill the north, and a smell of
snow pervades the air.

The Professor has broached a scheme for keeping tab on the
horses all night. We are to divide into watches. He cut five willow
twigs, and we have drawn lots. Fred is to watch from 9 to 11; the
Professor from 11 to 1; Simon, 1 to 3; I, 3 to 5; Miller, 5 to 7, while
cooking breakfast. Then we'll start up the pass! Miller and I think
that we should reconnoitre here to-morrow, and that the Professor
is working his faith-in-God-and-self, and line-of-least-resistance
racket, a mite too strong.

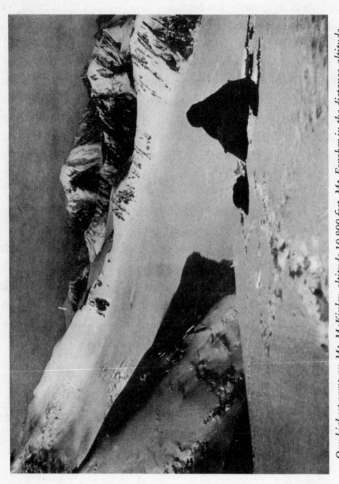

Our highest camp on Mt. McKinley, altitude 10,800 feet. Mt. Foraker in the distance, altitude 17,000 feet. Slopes of Mt. Hunter to the left.

CHAPTER XIX

WILLOW BUSHES TO AQUATICS

SEPTEMBER 8.—We went to bed by starlight. Fred watched o.k., but the talk at changing shifts, and at last a long confab of the Professor and Simon kept me awake. It was the kid's watch after his boss's. I could see them there by the fire. Some trouble was up. Ptarmigan swooping from place to place made a noise like a wheat thrasher in full blast.

The blind kid came to me for my Zeiss glasses, useless even on a dull day, and now scudding cloud hid the moon. "The horses have disappeared," said he. "The Professor-r-r wants me to go downstream to look." I said a few profane things.

I went to the fire. The Professor took shape out of the night. "Why, I went out to make sure the horses were there every little while," said he, childishly. "Three times I headed them off. They kept so still, I was sure it was they, but when I went over, it was only a willow bush!" Only a willow bush! I could have—but I didn't. So, the author of this fussy scheme was the very one to lose the beasts on his own watch, dreaming at the fire, having kept us awake all night. And then, instead of chasing the beasts himself, he went to bed, ordering his orderly to hunt. Simon was only too eager, know-ing he couldn't find them, so he could sleep at daylight while we hunted. And he expected me now to sit and wait by the fire, then hunt all day, too. We ought to have let the horses go for a while, half of us hunted them to-day, while the others "found the pass."

After enough sleep, the Professor's conscience began to work; he thought he ought to go hunting, and was up with me at daylight. Fred and Miller sensibly lay like logs. The Professor went down-stream, I up, without eating, nearly to the glacier, where a strange sulphurous smell, either from a rock vent or decaying sulphides, filled the air. No tracks. Back at camp, Miller was trying to light the fire, speechless with grouch. Downstream I followed the Professor, who soon appeared near the little creek flowing off the hill crossed yesterday, shouting something—he hadn't the horses, so I didn't care what. I went far below where we struck the stream, then back to where the Professor had stood, and right there were *tracks,* scat-tering up the hill, lost in the moss. He'd welched back to camp. Suppose he had seen and hadn't followed them! I boiled.

I trudged the three miles over to the big stream crossed yesterday—the logical, hard thing; walked a mile up and down its bed, searching the flats beyond. No traces: only sixty-eight sheep not half a mile off, eating the sunlight off the mountain. Returning, there was Fred, driving the lost beasts up our stream. At camp, he and Miller were pretty mad. What they said about the Professor as a watchman and horse-rustler would never do to write. But he hadn't seen any tracks at the creek. "Rub his nose in tracks, and he wouldn't see them," said Fred, who had found my tracks, but in-stead of back-trailing, had swung along the hill-top. "I found 'em on a scratch shot," said he.

"Back here," said Miller, "the Professor didn't seem to give a hang whether he had his horses or not. He just said, 'Tell Dunn and King to bring the outfit up the glacier to the pass when they find the horses.'" "Pass? What pass?" sneered Fred. "Why, with hungry horses lost like that, nothing but frozen grass anywheres, we ought to have expected to be here a week huntin', they might scatter so far. But no, I see with only a week's grub, and us on the wrong side of the mountains, he doesn't give a hoot about his pack train, and just starts up onto the ice with his orderly, Simon. H—l!"

We considered waiting there for the pass-finders, but felt more charitable after eating, and packed up, leaving behind for spite Simon's caribou skin.

So we drove the beasts up the long, hoof-grueling moraine, out upon clean ice. Ahead, the dazzling avenue swung east past a pyramidal white peak, whose nearer ridge met the glacier's left wall at a tiny nick. Forward loomed a serac; clouds scudded up from the north; we bungled on for an hour in a snowstorm, till the Professor and Simon glimmered atop the icefall, giants by mirage. Once more we played the old game of quadrilling upward among snow-choked crevasses in a blizzard, each tied to a horse for safety. Twice the Dark Gray and P.R. caved through and were roped out. Once Fred went under just where I had been standing.

The Professor had peeked through the nick before going to the glacier's end, and had seen light down a narrow valley. We neared the place. The ice rose in frozen combers on a little fan of upright slate needles, perhaps forty feet wide, joining in a hundred yards white pillars supporting Heaven, which you felt should tremble in the luminous scud. Somehow we dragged the beasts to its knife-like top. But a pass was there, indeed a pass! Elevation, 6,100 feet. Now and again, as with beating hearts we started down from this most fiendish zenith of Alaskan desolation, the dark chasm curved away below in a tremor of sunlight; now, across sheer walls monstrously patched with round névé and gully snow, quivered an unearthly gold; then, far, far beyond, a silver glimmer revealed green lowlands and translucent peaks, surely guarding the Pacific!

Save poor dumb beasts from such a descent again! Never were horses so punished, even in this land. One by one we wheeled them, switch-backed them, stoned them, hauled them, shouted ourselves hoarse at them, till the thin snow on the cruel talus was a ladder of blood. Unshipping their packs, they fell, bracing themselves. At one drop, the P.R. lost his head, dashing up and down a narrow shelf, his load under his stomach; then with blood-dripping legs, he balked half an hour, till I thought his bones must stay there. Ten mud holes on the tundra would not have roused such terror.

Yet in two hours we came down three thousand feet, to the first bite of unfrozen grass for a fortnight, to forget-me-nots and hare-bells in bloom, and a last winter's snowbank still shriveling under a clump of willows that were putting forth stillborn leaves. Here, south of the mountains, summer lasts longer, though the snow never melts, and spring was just coming to those bushes.

"There was a man in our town," we said at supper, but I made it "willow," instead of "bramble bush." Honor be, after all, to the Professor.

We're safe on the south side of the range.

SEPTEMBER 9.—Early we came upon a sizable stream flowing east, draining the range at right angles to its valleys. Miller had left his camera hanging on a bush, and climbed back to camp for it as we waited. Simon and the Professor drew guess-maps of the valley, then played Pythagoras very seriously in the river sand. Fred, sitting on a log, sez he to me, sez he, "Look at the Professor in them ragged clothes. With his trousers hitched up, his heels tight together, he looks jest like a ballet girl goin' on the stage. No, more like an overgrown boy lookin' fer a job, or a clown at a circus, with that little cap, an' his long hair."

Halfway from this point to Cook Inlet, and north of where we left its western tributaries last July to cross the mountains, the Sushitna forks. The water that carries its name fills the east side of the valley; the Chulitna River, the west, our side; while a low range squats between. Above the forks, the Chulitna is all unmapped and unexplored; no one knows even if it is larger or smaller than the Sushitna. We are either at the Chulitna headwater, or a tributary of it—it's impossible to tell, and makes no difference, as all these rivers split into scores of tentacles at their heads. As soon as we strike deep enough water, we'll leave our horses and raft for speed's sake; but that stream was still too shallow, and hadn't yet decided to turn south—our direction. We were sure it veers before long, for eastward we can see the far wall of the valley running straight south from the great range which we have just crossed, and the gap where the Sushitna and Cantwell headwaters meet.

Halfway to the forks, Government maps show two dotted parallel lines, marking a supposed huge glacier—probably seen from the Sushitna side of the valley, which has been explored—meeting the Chulitna from the south side of McKinley. We want to confirm and investigate this glacier. As the rainfall on this side of the mountains is much greater than on the north side, this ice river, if it exists, should be larger than Muldrow glacier, even if its watershed is smaller. Simon fondly pretends to imagine that we shall try to ascend McKinley by it. It is the glacier which the Professor, in his old day-dreams of success, declared we should follow on sleds in descending the mountain. Once he even hinted that we ought to lug runners to the top, to skid down upon!

So we left the stream, and struck southeast out into the valley, away from the mountains, over the sunbaked rocks of a big moraine, which showed that this river's course had once all been ice. Simon fell behind with me, chattering confidingly. His father makes paint, and sells a wonderful preparation (so he said) called—"something-oid," which you can use to roof the desert, mend holes in your head, heart, or cabin; it's bullet-proof, acid-proof, water-proof, fire-proof, God-and-devil-proof; and in every uncivilized part of the world pioneers bless it nightly with flesh sacrifices. Poor, practical, material Simon! He chattered on and on, as the tundra streams gathered into a torrent, and plunged us into canyons. He is going to devote his life to

booming and discovering new uses for "something-oid." This is sim-
plicity and enthusiasm for you—and money to be got.

At last sheer slate cliffs and the torrent's roar cast us upward to
camp, drenched and sore-hoofed. From our hill, we look down upon
an even larger source of the Chulitna, flowing straight east from the
cloudy northern precincts of McKinley, among labyrinthine sand-
bars and lines of saffron cottonwoods.

For supper, we've tried Labrador tea, having scarce a handful of
the real stuff left. Its ferny leaves, red and woolly underneath, taste
mild and old-maidish, and of the swamp.

SEPTEMBER 10.—Through strangling alders once more we slid
down to that big stream. One mile, and it swung due north, into a
great canyon. We followed.

Shall we ever get out of this cursed gorge? Again begins the old
game of fording and refording. All day, we watched that familiar
cartoon of humanity, the Professor, sprawling on the overloaded
Light Gray's rear, as we swung from bar to bar, ploughing every few
yards through a treacherous channel. Up leaped the cliffs to 400
feet sheer on both sides. It was swim or back trail, if we didn't like
it. Hour after hour the canyon twisted like a snake, so it seemed at
each bend that we must tunnel a way on. I pitied the poor shivering
brutes, with hoofs still mashed from that pass, unable to see the
stones that moiled them in the milk-white water—each of us on a
rump, making two and a half hundred pounds on all of five backs.

By noon, channels were so deep each ford was a swim. And resting at noon grub, I insulted fate, and have swallowed the consequences. I used Miller's pocket mirror to examine some pimples on
my face (from eating beans floating in moose-fat). Then I sat on the
mirror and broke it. So, soon after, as the horses crowded together
at the thousandth ford, the Whiteface got a bad hold on a bowlder
with his right hind foot; it slipped, and landed on my left, his whole
weight, plus the leverage of the other three hoofs used in scram-

The steep southwestern shoulder of Mt. McKinley (much foreshortened), our objective point. The "pink cliffs" to the left.

bling to regain his balance. I thought he'd hacked the foot off. But on I pottered, moaning, hopping, groveling, over two more swims, till the Professor made me take off my boot. There were the toes all right, but bloody and with big red gobs under the nails; and he wrapped them in his red bandanna.

Still we forded, each time having to swim further and further, until the Little Gray rolled over in mid-channel, shipping the Professor, who sprawled along, swept into a rapid under the slate cliffs. "He floats very high—from the air in his clothes, I guess," said Fred calmly, looking on. That brought the man sense to call a halt. Still, we had one more channel, and that nearly did for me. In mid-stream, and I perched behind his pack, pain, mashed toes and all, Whiteface stood a while upright, treading water with his hind legs, pawing the air with his front. The crowd thought he'd topple over; he ought to have, and if he had—

I've hopped on one leg to this bar camp. Everything is sandy and soaked. Our clothes are falling to pieces, our boots are worn out; mine are a cast-off pair of Miller's. I've been sitting still an hour, sick at my stomach, moaning, swearing, biting my shirt from pain. Not a blade of grass down here, and stuck in this canyon, we can't get the beasts up these stage back-drop cliffs. Fred has just climbed them, and reports swamps, lakes, and confused tributaries ahead—making it impossible to travel up there—and no break in our gorge. We've no idea how far we are from the sea, what falls or rapids may be ahead, whether the water fills the canyon completely, as it may, and checkmate us. This is making Cook Inlet in two days from crossing the pass, as the Professor prophesied and Miller bet, with a vengeance. We haven't started down this immense valley. Bets are that we'll abandon the horses to-morrow.

The Professor is trimming Fred's whiskers into a vandyke. It's nearly dark. Drying fires twinkle in the willows; over one, Simon is giggling and waving his wet college flag. We're soaked in caribou grease; we eat so much we exude it. The Abney level is drying in the reflector. We're making sarcastic remarks about the existence of that big glacier.

Miller shouts from the fire, "How late's the barber shop open?" And it's beginning to rain.

SEPTEMBER 11.—Not a wink of sleep last night, from the foot pain, and the hungry beasts pawing and tramping ceaselessly four inches from our heads. Right after starting, the canyon narrowed, so we had to ford every forty feet or so. And every channel was a swim. We covered about a quarter mile an hour.

Most packers will tell you that it's impossible to ride a swimming packed horse. If he once turns turtle, he can't right himself; his pack's too heavy, and generally swings under his stomach. You must slip off then, escaping the splashy play of his hoofs, if you can. Unless he's washed ashore on a bar, he drowns, and the pack's lost.

Again and again all the morning, we just escaped. Your beast stands upright, circling downstream, treading water, ready to topple over, till the current eases, or a hoof strikes a bowlder safely. We kneeled on the haunches, like circus-riders, frantically wigging an ear, banging a neck, blinding an eye with one hand, as your shivering, overloaded beast snorts in the icy mud-water, and your eyes play about on the racing shore line, and the whirlpool sneaks toward you, up through the humming rapid under the cliff. The Professor began to hop round like a puppet, trying to choose fords where the current shot you just right to still water on the other shore, so you might, or might not, escape the foam collars. And all in the rain.

Of course it was madness. Spruces a-plenty for rafts grew in rock clefts, but halt and build them the Professor would not. Why? Just pig-headedness. He said that the water wasn't deep enough for rafting. "There's rafting water for you," said Miller at each crossing. "A schooner'd float from here to the Inlet without scratchin'," Fred would mutter. But we were too engrossed and excited to revolt. The game was capturing our blood. From dreading, pausing, talking fast and nervously, waiting for the first man to plunge in at each swim, we began to dash in all together and carelessly, with the intoxication you get from having survived too often when you shouldn't. Of course, the slow-blooded Professor responded cumbrously to this stimulant. He began to value life after we had forgotten it. Toward noon, an earth bank replaced a cliff, and we scrambled up to the valley level, traveling east a while from the river.

Two miles, and the stream followed and headed us; so we plunged down between gravel banks, to where it flowed openly over bars all the afternoon. Late, a large clear stream emerged on the left (east). And again the slate canyon cliffs menace ahead.

We've come perhaps six miles to-day. Camp's in the rain here, a mile below the tributary. For the first time since leaving Peters glacier the tents are up. Simon and I have just batted the poor beasts up the alder-covered wall of the gorge, where some miracle may have grown feed. Camp-fire is between two little spruces in the oozy river muck, just big enough for three to huddle over, while the others stand and shiver. Too wet and chill to write.

One thing's sure: we can't take horses down this river-bed to the big mythical glacier. To-morrow'll be worse than to-day. I've just told the Professor so. He simply went on eating, not even winked. Of course he's never told us in so many words that he intends driving the pack train to the glacier, but has often given that impression. He gives nothing but impressions; you have to be a mind-reader to draw him out. Still none of our plans or intentions are put into words, still we grope along in the dark. Certainly, we're losing by not rafting, to say nothing of the silly risk. And if time is no object, it's sure possible to take the beasts slowly across the box canyons and small stream gorges of the valley level. Any way is less stubborn and childish than this sloshy, amateur hippodroming.

SEPTEMBER 12.—Still the swimming game, which now seems to amuse the Professor so; still rain. Never before has the outfit been so soaked and demoralized. Still the canyon, and the second ford was a long swim.

All but Simon had crossed circus-fashion, kneeling on his horse's haunch behind the pack. We turned to watch the kid on the Big Gray, last as usual. He was cavorting backward in circles, with a good list, downstream under the cliffs. "Jump! Swim!" we shouted to him, but still he clung to the wall-eyed beast, whose pack slipped under his stomach, as he lurched on one side, all under water but his waving heels. Simon appeared a goner. Finally, where the water boiled worst, the boy seemed to get free of the horse, struggling with his rubber cape. And he escaped the heels, swimming, and to our amazement dragged himself out on a ledge of the 500-foot cliff, but it was on the wrong shore.

Away floated the Gray, rolling, snorting, plunging down the swift water, arching up his neck less and less for a grunt of air, his nose under water. Fred and I dashed down the bar to grab him, in case he touched an eddy on our shore. But we thought he was done for— with my camera, sweater, mackinaw, and Tom Sawyer aboard; when slyly he did strike a backwater, righted himself, and stood up bewildered and dripping, a water-logged statue.

Simon, unable to climb around the cliff, was stripping to swim. The Professor from our side did the same, to rescue Simon, I suppose, while Fred and I hugged the background to let the man get a dose of the fruit of his own fording medicine. But the kid pluckily dived and swam the current, his duds tied around his neck, before the hesitating Professor was wet to the knees. He made shore a hundred yards below us, as Miller dashed out into the current, gallantly throwing him a coiled cinch line.

My pent indignation broke loose. I asked the Professor if rafting wasn't now "following the line of least resistance." (Fred whispered sarcastically at my side, "Holler about not wantin' to abandon this nice pack outfit yet, so he will quit it; he goes so by opposites.") Silence. His stubbornness, no sense of humor, unsensitiveness to the hurts of man and beast, awful self-seriousness—all are amazing. He wouldn't even stop to build drenched Simon a fire, and Simon complained to me. For once I pitied the poor kid, clattering over the stones on the run for warmth. I told him that he stood too much from the Professor. But think of his orderly's kicking! And still we forded and reforded the deadly channels.

We set a drift-pile ablaze at noon. Right after, the river made amazing twists, and having spared us in another bad swim, the current grew narrower and swifter than ever before, butting into the cliffs at right angles with a good whirlpool under. The Professor halted and began talking about taking too much risk, with Miller and King unable to swim. I said that I'd try the place, though it was worse than Simon's Scylla; that since we'd swam so far, we might as well keep on swimming. The Professor hemmed and hawed quite seriously; up to now he'd pretended to take all our aquatics as a huge joke. He sidled over to Miller, and smirked, "How would you like to ford a horse here, if you can't swim?" That made me hot. "Of course, Miller'll follow wherever you lead," I said. "How can you ask him that? His swimming a horse here is a question for you to decide, not Miller." Only more hemming and hawing for answer; gazing sleepily at the timber, and a wonder "if the horses can get out of the canyon." Then the Professor's inevitable procrastinative, "Well, camp anyhow, and we'll see." . . .

Half the sugar has seeped away, and the syrupy sack is squashed flat. The beans are swollen and sprouting. The last baking-powder tin had only two teaspoonfuls of a brown liquid, which faintly inspired the last reflector-full of bread, which when cooked you couldn't bite even after soaking. It's filled with chunks of green mildew, like currant cake. No tea at all. I've kicked the reflector off into the brush (we've nothing more to bake) without obsequies. The caribou and moose meat's dumped out into the sand in the rain—at a safe distance from camp—since each chunk is deeply shaved before it's edible. Kerosene, mildew, horse-sores, and a week's soaking make our blankets fit to please some Paul Verlaine.

I'm in the tent, which smells something like a stable—the Augean one before what's-his-name flushed it. The bushes about the fire groan under wet and rotten socks, pants, coats, all getting wetter. The rain falls in great gobs from the yellow cottonwoods. The starved horses are crashing about in the brush. I can see four sullen human beings, hands behind backs, backs to the fire, not a soul uttering one word.

Simon has been hollering once more about throwing away chances to climb McKinley by abandoning the horses. He laid it on stronger than ever before, and the bluff was more transparent. No one paid any attention to him but the Professor, to whom the kid must be our indefatigable hero. Now he's talking about the specific gravity of cottonwood; Miller about how unwieldly a raft of it would be; Fred about how it's sure death to swim a pack horse more than thirty feet. No sound but the patter of rain and the incessant roar of this rock-walled river, flowing only God knows where....

At last the Professor's pig-head is snagged! To-morrow, so he says, we're to build rafts; not of spruce, which is best, but of the big cottonwoods over camp. We might just as well have rafted in the beginning, and been at the mythical glacier three days ago.

Lord! There's the kid making another holler about quitting the horses, offering to drive them down the canyon behind the rafts with us aboard!

SEPTEMBER 13.—Early the river-bed began shaking with the fall of eighty-foot cottonwoods—whiz, zizz, crash! Fred was chopping in the rain at dawn, and all day we've been rolling logs to the whirlpool back-water, on all kinds of clumsy rollers and skids devised by the Professor.

He was so nifty at this, that as we pawed along logs with our hands, bent double in the quicksand, I said, "You must have worked in a lumber yard once." "I really don't know that I ever have," he answered seriously, and offended. Worst was rolling them out through shallow water and foamy stones to mid-channel, to drift to the pool. Simon and the Professor of course shied at getting their feet wet and Miller lost the first log he guided, getting in over our only rubber boots. He took them off and went to work again, but the other two now wouldn't even work with them on. Rubber boots are a dreadful affectation; once I get them, in they go to the old Chulitna.

Through the afternoon every one but yours truly appointed himself a Herreshoff, and gave orders to Fred, who notched the logs. Miller especially assumed an air of touch-me-not importance, being an amateur Puget Sound sailor. Y. t. retired to camp to dry the dregs of the food, as the rain had stopped, and took the liberty of naming the raft *Mary Ann*—accepted in the face of Miller's suggested *Reliance*, and Simon's *Discovery*.

Now at dusk she rocks large, green and clumsy in the whirlpool ways. The Professor has climbed the bench, and seen nothing in the fog. Yet squatting here over our beans swimming in grease, our meat fried to leather to kill the fetor, he has found a mind again, and announces that as the river "may be straighter" from the terrace-top, the horses will be driven on another day or two, while Miller and King, the non-swimmers, will speed the raft. Simon, of course, had to volunteer to stick by the beasts, having hollered so much about quitting them. I could do as I chose, and having decided a week ago, wrapped my meagre duffle in a tarpaulin, and said, "Raft."

CHAPTER XX

SWIFT WATER INTO
GREAT GLACIERS

SEPTEMBER 14.—After grease and beans, we began sorting the outfit; grub and duffle, wet already, for *Mary;* junk and botany cases for the horses. I find the beasts and load with the Professor.

Everything's ready—when up hike Fred and Miller from the whirlpool, and give the raft a black eye; wouldn't even hold three men, let alone any stuff, weighs over three ton, too heavy to handle anyhow, and you'd never get her off if you grounded. The soaked green cottonwood was pretty low in the water, but no worse than I foresaw. She looked able to take two men and a few other pounds, at least, said I. Every one stampeded to her, danced on her, looked wise and shook his head. Protest as I would, she was condemned.

Fred and I piled everything pell mell on the brutes, and I got Whiteface ready to be my water chariot again. "We'll try the horses swimming this channel, anyway," said the Professor, with usual evasion of the main issue. "See how they go, and if it's all right, take the ropes off the raft to make one below, where there's dry spruce. I think that will be the solution of our problem." If the beasts didn't ford all right, I wondered what the "solution" to the "problem" would be, but held my tongue.

The Professor on Little Gray, then Big Buck, Simon on the Roan—carried down to the whirlpool, but hanging on—and the other four beasts did cross safely. King, Miller and I went down to the raft to get its ropes, as I thought. Says Fred, looking at her, "I'll try her if you will." "I'm willing," answers Miller. "She'll be a fright, though," grins Fred. Miller guesses that she will. "The horses is all right, ain't they?" asks King, looking at Whiteface, alone on this side the channel. "Oh, sure," answers Miller, unlashing *Mary*, and jumping aboard with Fred. Out they swing, warding off the sheer wall with poles, away and free, safely across the whirlpool, smoothly down with the quaking current, out of sight!

I was mad enough. But the Whiteface had to be forded; I knew that and so did they, and I can swim. So, the raft's black eye was a put-up job—but could you blame them? They'd have been drowned if thrown from horses into that current. How else could they get around the Professor's order for all to swim again? For plainly the raft wouldn't have held another pound, and, once approved of, the Professor would have loaded her.

I plunged into the current aboard Whiteface, worst water-horse that is. He started well enough, but halfway across turned suddenly, swimming downstream. Yanking the halter rope, banging his right eye, wouldn't budge him. Right at the pool-edge I was ready to slip off, when I grabbed both ears, and nearly pulling them up by the roots, twisted his head up, and pointed it ashore. He took the hint, and in a moment grounded. Narrow squeak.

Another swim, longer but in quieter water, where the beast stood on his hind legs awhile treading water, and we passed a turn in the stream. There were King and Miller sitting ashore on the stranded raft. A large clear stream met our river from the west. Did it flow from the mythical glacier? It shouldn't, being clear, though sometimes ice-fed channels lose their silt late in the year. Anyhow, spruces should grow up its valley. That impressed the Professor, who, having "worked out our position" with a stick and compass, and admitted that with this added water it would be suicidally foolish to keep on fording, agreed to follow up the fork.

Camp is under a bank where dead spruces a-plenty grow. The Professor and I, in stolid silence, monkeying with the Abney level, have just climbed the "eminence" back of camp—as he calls the butte of slate left by the creek's erosion. Plainly it flows from no near glacier (the mysterious one is mapped as planting its ice only a few miles from the main Chulitna), but bears off N. 70° W. into cloud-capped foot-hills. Yet over a ridge southwest, S. 60° W., we saw what may be our longed-for valley, though walled from us by the bluish outlines of immense mountains, in layer after layer.

It's only five miles from us, air line, says the Professor, but I call it quite a dozen. How he can deceive himself when he wants to! I suggested hitting thither overland, but he disagreed, fearing box canyons. He was apathetic, discouraged. I got a mess of cranberries.

SEPTEMBER 15.—Raft-building; packing heavy logs on sore shoulders, stumbling down bench after bench through alder jungles, to the ways. Every now and then Miller disappears importantly with the axe—he's our naval architect—and comes back with a little green spruce tree. The Professor fusses about, whittling off knots with a pen-knife. Simon mopes by the fire, reading the Professor's red survey book. Fred works....

Two rafts are ready for launching, one *Mary Ann II,* the other, *Ethel May,* named by Miller for a friend of his in Seattle, "of whom," as Bret Harte would observe, "perhaps the less said the better."

Now all the salt is gone. After yesterday's swim, only a little brine slopped in the can. We've begun on the last white beans, just half a sack, which taste slimy with no salt, and we all shy from the meat.

The Professor says that salt eating is only a habit, unnecessary for health or digestion. "From the way he talks, I believe he wanted to get rid o' all our salt," says Fred, who suffers much without it. The pea-soup powder is all slime. The mildewed evaporated onions which Simon cooked for supper were great. Miller is rendering more grease. Shoulders are raw and backs ache from packing and skidding logs.

The cottonwoods along the bars are saffron and orange, above on the tundra the brush is dizzy scarlet, in the swales the six-foot grass is mashed and brown; only the lean sombre spruce, scattered through the colorful desolation, so changeless all the year, puts balance and order into nature delirious with coming death. There are no mosquitoes; now no rain; warm, sunny days, icy nights; the haunting sub-bass of the dwindling streams chants ceaselessly that being is without end or purpose. It's the North I love.

SEPTEMBER 16.—Rotting clothing and rotted food all sorted, we launched our crafts. I carried the pack saddles, up the terrace, and cached them under a birch. For near two days, we have seen no horses. We did not find them now, to say good-bye—or shoot. No one mentioned them. We just forgot them, in a guilty conspiracy of silence. I've already explained and tried to excuse such cowardice. Here they have no chance to live. The snow in this valley gets too deep for rustling grass; weakening, wolves will kill them.

Simon pottered over his dunnage for just two hours, while I pondered these equine obituaries:

> BROWN B: He was the one cayuse
> Labor with dignity to fuse.
> Never to curse him was your hunch
> (Though always scattering the bunch).
> But rather plead, "Highness, you err,
> "Please return to the trail,"

Or, "Excuse me, you fail
"To note our direction, kind sir."
For when in homely oaths you blamed,
He gave you a look, and you felt ashamed.

WHITEFACE: He was Brown B's chum.
Hated work, but kept it mum.
Into mud-holes he would slip,
Just to wag his lower lip.
    Sink in the roots?
      Never he;
His hoofs were made for fourteen boots,
    To extricate him cleverly.
Trailing, he seemed to say, "Here I am,
Plugging along, not giving a damn.
Always last in the line. Don't worry. See?
And for Sam Hill's sake, *never* hurry me."

BIG BUCK: It was a shame to force
So old and reverend a horse
To waltz through swamps, and eat the spray
Of glacier stream *cafe au lait.*
I know he felt it quite below
His dignity to be served so;
Yet he deserved no better fate
Because his brains were not first rate.
Also, he had a horrid knack
When you were fording on his back,
Of bucking feebly, as to scatter
Your limbs and dunnage in the water. (*Noble rhyme!*)
His mates he bullied on the trail,
And he chawed all the skin off the stump of the Whiteface's tail.
   (*Alexandrine.*)

Rhymes are getting low. Still, here goes:

P.R. SORREL bore the curse
Of Simon's botany. What's worse?
So all the other beasts refused
To browse with him. "We're not amused,"
Said they, "Your job we don't admire,
Get out, you Ghetto-bred pariah—
Go stand beside your own smudge-fire."
He was an outcast from the herd,
But as a pack horse? Oh, a bird.
If ever cayuse bore a cross,
Did poor P.R. (At a dead loss.)

This aged ROAN, too, had spunk,
Sometimes he packed our crates of junk,
And aptly chose to raise the devil
With aneroid and Abney level.
Had he been wise to mica-schist
He might have been a scientist,
Yet kept he with the wolves his tryst,
Unmindful of the fame he missed.

The brothers GRAY were worth their salt,
With many virtues and one fault.
Each snow-bridges would safely leap,
Unmindful of the crevasse deep,
And still a perfect balance keep.
Though to our leader hitched by rope,
Behind his khaki rear to grope,
LIGHT balked not on the steepest slope.
Yet DARK one grievous error would have
Rectified that time he should have
Drowned our Simon when he could have.

At eleven o'clock to-day began the most thrilling sport I know—
rafting down the snaky canyons of an unmapped glacier river.

Fred and I captained *Mary Ann II,* the other three *Ethel May.* We rasped and hauled them over the gravel shallows of our tributary, and shot out between the main walls of the stream, seizing on that boiling current. We reached silently from cliff to cliff, jammed pike-poles into the slate shelf overhead, twirled out of eddies. Entering creeks shattered the sheer wall. We chose the wrong channel, and it petered out. We bumped and grounded. We dashed overboard, and on the run eased her across shallows. We tugged half an hour to make an inch at each shove through the gravel, suddenly plunged in to our necks, and she leaped free as we scrambled on.

Bowlders rose through white ruffs of water in mid-channel. We might, or might not, hang on them for a perpendicular minute. Safely past they heaved and roared, like harbor-buoys breasting the tide. Sudden granite made gateways, pinching the river in its jaws, which quite filled them. Butte-like islands choked them, each crowned with two spare spruces on high. We rolled between, close to the mainland wall, like peas down a drain.

Still the cliffs narrowed, and we rocked through tunnel-like places, cool with dripping edges, which made a heart-sick barrier ahead, till, at the moment for shouting out, the walls magically slipped in twain. We speed with an irresistible, chariot-racing turn around a black pinnacle—toward cataract or rapid—guess? We only drop four feet through a feather-white V, and loosed from the canyon, the river hisses upon silt bars—swings us centrifugally around great arcs, twirling under the alder bayonets of cut banks, that would impale and behead—crashing us over giant logs that nodded solemnly up and down, up and down, as if pendulums keeping tab on the river's life in the measures of eternity.

Choosing different channels, hitting rapids at different angles, loitering along eddies, we alternately outrun one another. We see the *Ethel* only in the moment she flashes past, her three figures standing rigid. Then they are beyond by a whole universe, which is the ten feet of enchanted, wet, black satin around our log.

You must be very handy with a pole. You must have a hair-fine eye for moving angles, strength of an eddy, strike of a cross-chop, depth of foam ruffling over a stump. You must be surer of the length of your pole than a polo-player of his mallet's reach. You must know, just as a frog foretells rain, how many times between this drift-pile and that eddy your raft must swing, that the dead water may catch its hind end right; how long momentum will hold you, to twist the fore end to catch the riffle six yards beyond, so you just shave the bowlder in mid-channel, swinging straight from a broadside. You must be quicker than a Siwash dog. You must know the different weight of each log down to ounces, the balance of the duffle piled high like a dais, covered with the tent and the bean-pot, the mackinaws and the axe lashed to all the lashings. It's a pretty game.

Having one cook outfit, one raft has to wait for the other at grub times. *Ethel* waited for us at noon. Landing a raft is something like circus hoop-riding. You pick an eddy head (chances are it's a riffle) and one man stands ready with the stern rope, one with the bow-line. One jumps as the water shallows, making for shore, dragged along as he hauls in, easing Mr. Raft for the other man, who tumbles over now for a haul in unison. And if you've missed the eddy, or the current's too swift, no rope and pole may hold her; or if they will, the rip may turn her turtle.

Early this afternoon we scraped through our underlashings running over shallows, and nearly dissolved before hauling safe into an eddy. Luckily we were ahead, for otherwise *Ethel*'s crew might have slept hungry, as we carry the pots. If we divided grub between the rafts, each's share would be too small to see, we have so much left; and we might never meet again, for now we're once started, with twenty miles to the good in three hours, not a ton of chewing plug on the beach could keep Fred from hot-footing to Cook Inlet. He believes we're almost there. D—n that glacier.

When the *Ethel* slid into camp to-night, Miller comes to me and sez he, in his bass whisper, "You ought to see Simon. Whenever we pass a bad place, he jumps up and down, and yells, 'Professor-r-r, you're the captain, remember, Professor-r-r.' " After supper, comes Simon, giggling, and sez he, "Dunn, you ought to see Miller whenever we take a sharp turn. He jumps around prophesying falls ahead, and wants to land and explore!" I should like to be on that raft about ten minutes—no more—and see the Professor wield a pike pole. I don't understand how he ever got to camp here. As for falls, gravels should have filled up any but a huge displacement of the river-bed in this glaciated valley.

Nothing but chunks of lignite to burn on this mid-river bar. Good night. We're getting home.

SEPTEMBER 18.—Shipyarding all yesterday morning—the first day I've written no diary.

A low, yellow cottonwood forest reached far back as we could see from the river's west shore, just opposite camp. Thinks the Professor, "There is a short cut to our glacier, which must lie yonder." He and I try to ford the channels thither on foot, but they foam up and twirl our underpinnings before we're twenty yards from the bar, and we give up the reconnoissance. Yet were we so far wrong?

Toward noon *Mary Ann II* was all laced up again, and we pushed off. In a mile, we dance down past a cut gravel bank hanging out over us. The air is suddenly cool, and the gravels are very drippy. I jab my pole up into the wall, and though the top is dense with cottonwoods, mind you, I chip off a piece of ice. That bank was hard as a rock. Ice! Another mile, and we shot out among a thousand bars and channels, a flat quite two miles across. Northeast it swung toward the foothills, where debouched over a low piedmont what might have been a tongue of the old Gobi desert—the unmapped glacier at last! The icy gravel bank, of course, was an old moraine, left by the glacier as it has retreated, but too huge to melt, even in hundreds of short summers, more than to form soil and grow trees on its top.

Right off, Simon, the Professor, and I left King and Miller with the rafts, and taking two days' pemmican from our emergency grub, headed to explore the glacier. All the afternoon we tottered through its river's channels, slept on its west bank in the cotton-wood forest, still miles below the terminal moraine.

To-day, dawn found us hiking around its big brown pot-hole, where the tiny cottonwoods shriveled out. The monster is five miles broad, if an inch. We tackled the moraine. Sheer cones towered fifty, a hundred feet overhead, and we floundered, making zigzag goat-trails mid-high on their sliding sides. Surface cataracts trickled ceaselessly into the opal-blue water of cup-shaped abysses, violating the dead silence of such chaos as I have never seen. A man-sized river roared under its south border, between growing mountains and our walls of black ice; dove into the earth, foamed up, and dove again.

By noon, three miles of ice had choked this stream, and we reached a side gully in the mountains near its course. Here were old friends—willow bushes half withered, half in bud, blue-bells in bloom, and a last year's snowbank. Even robins still hopped about. Straight overhead rose an alp, around which the brown ice avenue twists south.

We could see more from this mountain than by following the glacier, so we climbed it to be checked by a ruff of slate at six thousand feet—and a view to make your hair curl.

The greatest of inland glaciers spread below. Flat and black, yet unribbed with white ice for many, many miles, this imperial avenue sent out here one scythe-shaped arm, there another, coiling in forty sheer miles to the golden snow clouds veiling McKinley. Imagine an octopus, or rather a mille-pus, to be pressed levelly into the valleys of all Switzerland. That's what we saw—there where human eye nor living organism has ever rested.

We are boiling pea soup at the snowbank, over the little alcohol stove. We are chatting like friends. Good night.

SEPTEMBER 19.—Struggling back to the rafts, all among the glacier cones this morning, Simon and the Professor began talking of men they had traveled with in the Arctic; the virtues of this one, the failings of that. Companions with the more endearing human traits they condemned, because such were not even-tempered and easygoing. So-and-so was too talkative. (Think of such an angel of light for the Arctic, spurned!) So-and-so was very charming at first, told stories very well, but you found out after a while that his enthusiasm was not real, and he trod on other people's religious prejudices. Selfishness did not seem to be a fault in their eyes, provided a man kept his mouth shut, and followed his leader in smiling. I felt I should like to be on one of this pair's ideal Arctic parties—for about a day.

"Don't you think," I asked the Professor, "that the leader who rouses personal devotion and enthusiasm in his men, though he may be sometimes unfair and his temper quick, will reach the Pole before the easy-going, forbearing, colorless sort?" "Dunn, your sort of leader would have to be an angel, too," said the Professor. "Well, then only an angel will reach the Pole," said I.

Back at the rafts, Fred had shaved off his hobo beard, and Miller had whittled a couple of paddles.

At once we pushed off. At once the river went to the devil in channels. Sometimes *Mary* and *Ethel* were abreast, with a half-mile bar between; sometimes three miles apart. Once, thinking that we were far ahead, Fred and I waited an hour for the others on a wooded island lately ripped in twain by the river, the channel choked with timber, till we gave *Ethel* up for wrecked. We kept on, looking for a camping-place, intending to walk back to the others with our one axe, which we had aboard, and help them rebuild.

But channel divided into channel, till scraping down a narrow ditch, Bang! a couple of logs bridging it tried to decapitate our load; held us there on edge, nearly swamping. Chopping through those logs was like sitting on a tree branch while cutting it off—we couldn't stand on the raft—and when we crashed through free, and the current took her, we leaped on the craft like bareback riders.

Then suddenly we slid out on a wide current, swinging east, around the low ridge which we think separates us, the Chulitna, from the Sushitna. Behind rose McKinley and Foraker, unearthly exhalations, all under the autumn sky of lacquered gold. "Look, look!" I cried, "it's another glacier!" and there another Gobi desert did burst the confines of the range.

It was dusk. Suddenly we heard voices on the bar, and landed in the first eddy seen for an hour. There was the *Ethel,* and ahead of us! Their channels had dwindled, too. "We thought once we'd have to take her apart, log by log, and portage," said Miller. It appeared that she had slipped under a sweeper, which Simon, standing on the load, had hurdled, circus-fashion. It had knocked the Professor overboard. Gosh, I wish I'd been there to see!

The wet botany truck is strewed all over the sand. We're postmorteming the day, shivering in the biting wind that swoops down from that glacier, huddled around the burning end of a huge drift log. Too tired to cook, to eat anything but the emergency pemmican, and stumble to bed on the hard, wet silt. Surely we're almost at the Sushitna.

CHAPTER XXI

HUMANITY AND HAPPINESS

SEPTEMBER 20.—Still we plunged east, at right angles across the valley, around the bare granite hills. The channel puckered narrower and narrower—into another black canyon. *Ethel* was ahead, just inside its jaws. Suddenly Simon shouted, pointing to the black rim of rock between water and cliffs.

"Tent! tent!" he cried. "See the stove pipe! Siwash dogs!"

And there, as if washed ashore from the black mill race, was a smoking log hut, too, and a whole lay-out of sluices.

We whistled and shouted. Two men in blue shirts and rubber boots appeared walking carelessly up-shore. The very light-haired one—Swede, of course,—gave a faint, cheerful whoop, and his black-haired little partner with the prospector's bulging eyes pointed out the eddy to swing into.

We landed, waiting for them to speak. I suppose that our failure, forgotten in this joy and those quick, homeward dashes, silenced us unconsciously.

"Which way did you come?" asked the dark man. "By the Tokashitna?" That river was a new one on us. We had missed it.

They said that we had passed its mouth just below the second big glacier. But wasn't the Chulitna quite unexplored? Yes, until they had ascended it this summer, as far as where we built our rafts, it appeared. Indians had told them of the Tokashitna.

Then we told them, but quite carelessly, in perhaps a hundred words, that we had been spending the summer about Mt. McKinley. We asked, between sentences, if they had salt or flour to spare. The Professor had the nerve to say that we had fresh meat to trade for luxuries like that.

"Yes, we heard of your outfit and plans at Tyonek," they said. But they didn't ask if we'd reached the top of McKinley.

"Them Indians at Sushitna Station will go crazy when they see you," said the Swede—Chrest Hansen by name. "You're a hard-looking lot with them red bandannas tying up you' hair."

In the tent, they gave us sour-dough bread, and we ate it standing in that human smell of old sour-dough miners that I know so well; by the long, plain board table with pressed glass salt cellars on it, the box-board bunk and great wads of gray blankets, the leather valises with boards on top for seats; the alarm clock. It was great to feel yourself reading what might be somewhere near the right time of day.

They had been digging flour gold here since July; getting a stake, no more. They gave us salt and tobacco—a whole plug to Fred—but had no flour to spare. Hansen gave me a pipe. They actually accepted some of our moose meat; held it up laughing a little childishly, saying, "Sure, yes, we know," as we warned them to shave the outside, and not get their noses too near. They told in great detail how they had missed hitting a brown bear up the river last July....

"See me spit on the rocks," chuckled Fred, as we walked back to the raft. "I chew it, tin tags an' all. It'll take a h—l of a lot of chawin' till I catch up lost time on plugs."

Hansen told us that the canyon was fifteen miles long, safe to raft if we kept to the right, and its lower end was not a dozen miles from the junction with the Sushitna! Last June it had taken them two weeks in high water to rope its length up to there.

But we haven't made the forks to-night. We ran the canyon in two hours. Camped here on the bar, it's very cold. Yet we're only a hundred miles from the Sushitna trading store—civilization.

SEPTEMBER 21.—Right at the start to-day, the river hurled us through a whole archipelago—once staid, tree-covered flats, which it had lately severed into town-lots. We dodged *Mary Ann* among shreds of jungle quivering in the white water, slapped her against the logs, till she buried a side, and the dizzy angle freed us. Fred and I hopped about, giving orders, changing them, cursing each other after every escape.

We had luck, but *Ethel* didn't. Once, where we landed to wait for her, first thing we know, Simon comes kiting down the bar after the axe. Back half a mile, we found *Ethel* hung up slanting on a willow snag, water washing over the junk boxes, the Professor and Miller nursing their dry feet on her up-turned edge. Fred jumped in and hacked them out, and in a half hour, both rafts abreast, we swung out upon the broad, even channel of the Chulitna and Sushitna pulling together for Cook Inlet. Rafting was easy now.

Here we sit on our load, raised on two logs in the middle of the raft and covered with the tent. Now and then we wonder which channel to take among the large islands, and the river chooses for us. Sometimes we loiter along shore, roused to paddle furiously when the steely water hustles on suddenly, and we scrape over shallows. But channels make little difference now; every lead has water enough.

Fred is staining the river with tobacco juice; I am smoking Chrest Hansen's pipe. We swing slowly round and round, as air bubbles hiss up from the gray-green flood. "See the view change without you movin',," says Fred; and after silent intervals, "Beautiful! beautiful! beautiful!" They seem asleep on the other raft; the Professor, anyway.

Northwest, McKinley, Foraker, and the coronet-like Titan between which we discovered, rise ever higher over these limitless lowlands. Clean blue shadows glaze the deeps of the saffron cottonwoods. Riffles upon shallows far ahead snuffle delicately and distinct through the warm sunlight of Indian summer. We dip our paddles with neat care. We live utterly in the present.

I wonder, shall I ever return to so glorious a land, to such happiness?

SEPTEMBER 24.— This afternoon, we began to bet on the exact time by the Professor's watch when Sushitna Station would loom up. He and Miller studied every eddy. A long one, said they, stretched just above the Station, into which flowed Yentna river, which they had ascended to meet us last July. We were standing on our loads, shading our eyes, speaking very seldom.

Toward four o'clock, a ruined cabin slid out upon a terrace with a clay bank under, and below dories were ranked ashore in a long stretch of dead water. Then weathered huts were tumbled in long, dead grass sloping evenly to the river. Spires of blue smoke rose, and on an island opposite appeared frowsy Siwash huts, the whine of dogs, savage shouts, scarlet cloth on the heads of moving squaws.

A tall old man strolled up-shore with four white men's dogs. We pulled in toward him, and asked him—not if Jack, whom we had sent back so sick just eight weeks ago, had ever reached here—but the news of the world. He knew of nothing since August 10.

"But yer know the Pope's dead?" he drawled. "And them cardinals held a sort of political convention, where Gibbons he acted as a kind of boss, showin' them the American way, and they elected a new Pope, his man. Roosevelt, he's agreed to complain to the Tsar of Rooshia about them massacred Jews, and some one's killed that

Queen Dragon of Servia, tryin' to jump her claim to the throne. And Rooshia's goin' to fight the Japs. The' ain't much happened this summer." His heavy boots clattered over the stones as he followed us, but he did not look at our open mouths, or ask us one word....

We're sitting about a camp-fire in the dark on the beach just below Shorty's store. He is on a trip to Tyonek, and his squaw wife handles his keys. Prospectors don't usually care for squaw-men, except Shorty, who is nearly seven feet tall. The wife walks about aggressively timid, maintaining the respect of all these prospectors, which she has mastered. Her eight children she guards in her cabin. She has been selling Simon candy of the Lower Silurian Age.

Nearly all the cabins are occupied. Prospectors are coming into this valley for the first time. No strike has been made, no, but it's the last valley in Alaska still untouched. They have spent the late summer boating up their years' supplies from the head of the Inlet. Some have dogs, some hope to get them from somewhere before winter. They are the bedrock Alaskan article, the men to be first on the claims if an Eldorado is struck. They start their stampede the winter before, not in the spring, which is the tenderfoot way. Each has just waked from failure—in a rush camp, or looking for daily wages in Valdez. Again they take up the old, relentless, dream-trail to riches through the desolate and uncertain North. Human beings, at least, men after my heart! In Arizona, Oregon, South Africa, the Philippines, each has more than once risked his poor all, and lost, always lost. But now the Eldorado is at hand, in this Sushitna valley, here is the place. They may hand-sled their outfits up the river in March, making many double trips; but to what point each is still undecided. There's plenty of time yet to think.

They handle the few rocks I have picked up, asking the simple, penetrating questions of men who have learned geology only in the field, and with one idea, placer gold. They talk of porphyry, bull granite, and gravel wash. They trace wise, slow fingers across our sketch maps, asking advice where they should go, like children. But if we have not seen such and such a schist on this or that creek, with bedrock so deep, it settles *that* Eldorado. Climbing McKinley does not interest them at all....

A tall, gaunt man has just come from prospecting in Luzon. He is cursing that country with great ingenuity. It's worthless, apparently, because you cannot grow oats there; corn, either, which he took out to settle the fate of the tropics with. There the natives are so thick and starved they search the mountains at night with candles for lizards to eat, till the hills seem alive with fire-flies.

Silently we look up to Mount Sushitna, rising clear and lone over the glossy river and the unknown wilderness, which is bright with uncertain auroras.

A shadowy figure approaches. I hear the Professor's voice in my ear. He is talking about Jack. He has heard that some such man, still ill, out of grub, with stories of many wrecks from a raft on the Keechatna, reached here in August. He took our boat to Tyonek. That is very annoying. However, the Professor has secured another craft, and to-morrow we shall follow to the sea.

A NOTE ON THE TEXT

This Modern Library edition of *The Shameless Diary of an Explorer* was reset from the original 1907 edition. Obvious typographical errors, some inconsistencies in spelling and hyphenation, and minor, apparently inadvertent misstatements of fact have been silently corrected; in all other regards, the present text reproduces the original.

A NOTE ON THE TYPE

The principal text of this Modern Library edition
was set in a digitized version of Janson,
a typeface that dates from about 1690 and was cut by Nicholas Kis,
a Hungarian working in Amsterdam. The original matrices have
survived and are held by the Stempel foundry in Germany.
Hermann Zapf redesigned some of the weights and sizes for Stempel,
basing his revisions on the original design.